God's Tapestry

Also by W. Eugene March from Westminster John Knox Press

God's Land on Loan: Israel, Palestine, and the World

Great Themes of the Bible, Volume 1

The Wide, Wide Circle of Divine Love:
A Biblical Case for Religious Diversity

God's Tapestry

Reading the Bible in a World of Religious Diversity

W. Eugene March

WESTMINSTER
JOHN KNOX PRESS
LOUISVILLE · KENTUCKY

© 2009 W. Eugene March

Westminster John Knox Press
Louisville, Kentucky

09 10 11 12 13 14 15 16 17 18—10 9 8 7 6 5 4 3 2 1

Book design by Sharon Adams
Cover design by designpointinc.com

Library of Congress Cataloging-in-Publication Data

March, W. Eugene (Wallace Eugene), 1935–
   God's tapestry : reading the Bible in a world of religious diversity /
W. Eugene March.
      p. cm.
   Includes bibliographical references.
   ISBN 978-0-664-23360-0 (alk. paper)
   1. Christianity and other religions.   2. Religious pluralism.   3. Bible—
Criticism, interpretation, etc.   I. Title.
BR127.M285 2009
261.2—dc22
                                                                2008027991

PRINTED IN THE UNITED STATES OF AMERICA

♾ The paper used in this publication meets the minimum requirements
of the American National Standard for Information Sciences—Permanence
of Paper for Printed Library Materials, ANSI Z39.48-1992

Westminster John Knox Press advocates the responsible use of our natural
resources. The text paper of this book is made from at least
30% post-consumer waste.

In loving memory of my mom,
Helen

On that day the deaf shall hear
    the words of a scroll,
And out of their gloom and darkness
    the eyes of the blind shall see.
The meek shall obtain fresh joy in the Lord
    and the neediest people shall
    exult in the Holy One of Israel.
                                    (Isaiah 29:18–19)

"Our first challenge in America today is simply to open our eyes to these changes, to discover America anew, and to explore the many ways in which the new immigration has changed the religious landscape of our cities and towns, our neighborhoods and schools."
                        —Diana Eck, *A New Religious America*

Contents

Acknowledgments

This book began with the invitation to present The Currie Lectures at Austin Presbyterian Theological Seminary, January 2007, entitled "With Open Eyes and Listening Hearts." I am grateful to President Ted Wardlaw and the Austin Seminary Faculty, for the opportunity to return to a place I dearly love. The welcome was warm and stimulating. The privilege of joining the list of Currie Lecturers is one I will always remember.

The next phase in the refinement of this project was at Mo-Ranch, a Presbyterian Conference Center in the hill country of central Texas, in October 2007. The event, a Reflective Retreat, concentrated on the theme "Religious Diversity as the Gift of God." I offer thanks to David Jordan for the invitation to be there, to the Mo-Ranch staff, and to those who participated in the event, teaching me so very much by their presence.

The third phase came in February 2008, at First Presbyterian Church in Dallas, Texas, where I presented The Brown Lectures titled "Under the Banyan Tree." I owe thanks to Robert Shelton, who as Interim Pastor first offered the invitation, and to Joe Clifford, the current Pastor, and the church staff, who showed such warm hospitality. Further, I want to express a special word of thanks to Micki Rawlings for all her help.

Finally, thanks to all at Westminster John Knox Press, and especially David Dobson, who have encouraged me and facilitated this project. To have a publisher who shows such interest and assistance is of inestimable value. And of course, without my understanding and supportive wife, Lynn, I would never have finished the work.

Preface

Some years ago I received an unexpected phone call from my mother. She was clearly agitated and thought I would share her concern, a theological concern. She was agitated about the language that had been used in fashioning a prayer to God in a study book that she and other women in her congregation were using.

Now let me say a word about my mother before I go further. Most of her life she was a reasonably reliable and consistent church worker. She did her share of teaching children in the church school. She cooked an untold number of casseroles and washed millions of dishes for the endless church socials that she helped to organize and attend. For many years she sang in the choir, listened to myriad sermons (some good, many more only so-so), and watched the clock, eager to get out at least a few minutes earlier than the other Christians heading for the Sunday specials at the local eateries. For some years she was an elder and served as clerk of the session of the small congregation to which she belonged. She did not think of herself as particularly "smart," but you could count on her if you were in need. In other words, my mom was a rather typical Christian woman who spent a great deal of time in or around her church.

But back to her phone call. The issue was a prayer in which feminine metaphors were employed to describe God's love for Israel. Wombs, labor pains, and nursing at nurturing breasts were used in a prayer to God. When Mom and her Bible study friends read this prayer, the explosion was not pleasant. And not surprisingly, an unofficial "denominational" publication circulating widely in her congregation fanned the fire of my mother's zeal to denounce perceived heresy.

It took me several minutes to get her calmed down enough for us to talk reasonably. When I did, I asked her to read the offending prayer to me. As she did, I recognized the clear influence of Isaiah. I said, "Hey, Mom, that language is straight out of the Bible."

She said, "It is not!"

I said, "Yes it is!"

"Is not!"

"Is too."

Finally, I asked her to get her Bible and we had a long-distance Bible study of some selected verses from the book of Isaiah:

> For a long time I have held my peace,
> I [God] have kept still and restrained myself;
> now I will cry out like a woman in labor;
> I will gasp and pant.
>
> Isaiah 42:14

> Can a woman forget her nursing child,
> or show no compassion for the child of her womb?
> Even these may forget,
> yet I will not forget you.
>
> Isaiah 49:15

> Rejoice with Jerusalem, and be glad for her,
> all you who love her;
> rejoice with her in joy,
> all you who mourn over her—
> that you may nurse and be satisfied
> from her consoling breast;
> that you may drink deeply with delight
> from her glorious bosom.
> For thus says the LORD:
> I will extend prosperity to her like a river,
> and the wealth of the nations like an overflowing stream;
> and you shall nurse and be carried on her arm,
> and dandled on her knees.
> As a mother comforts her child,
> so I will comfort you;
> you shall be comforted in Jerusalem.
>
> Isaiah 66:10–13

After she had read those verses, there was a long pause, and then she said, "When did they put that in there?" "It's been there all along," I replied. "Well," my dear mother continued in a somewhat subdued tone, "why didn't anyone ever tell me?"

"Why didn't anyone ever tell me?" That is one of the questions that prompted this book. There are so many misconceptions about what the Bible does say and doesn't say, so much ignorance among otherwise well-educated, capable people. In my experience, the people in the pews are often well ahead of the clergy when it comes to the matters that really count in the way we order our daily lives and structure the communities in which we live. Their attitudes are usually based on what they recognize from their own experience of life. But they need knowledge about the support the Bible can offer and encouragement and permission from their leaders. They often think that what they believe must be heretical or offbeat, since no one assures them otherwise.

Leaders, official and unofficial—pastors, church school teachers, youth leaders, officers, every serious follower of Jesus Christ—need to be informed on important issues and then speak clearly to those who look to them for guidance. Gender language is but one of numerous concerns we should address, but we need to do it in light of what the Bible actually says. For too long too many have claimed to speak the "truth" on the basis of faulty or little knowledge of the Bible. "Why didn't anyone ever tell me?" is a question that my mom should not have had to ask!

The Issue to Be Addressed

In this book "diversity" is the issue that will be explored. Political correctness is not the driving pressure. Rather, we seek theological clarity about how to deal with the realities of diversity we encounter in our communities: our schools, our workplaces, our political parties, our markets, our recreational facilities. Diversity is all around us: gender differences, racial and ethnic communities with a variety of languages, a wide divergence of social arrangement. Such differences are very much a part of our local and especially our international worlds. Any aspect of diversity is worthy of careful consideration, but this book will address one particular matter, the reality of religious diversity.

The Structure of the Discussion

Setting the stage for our explorations will be done in part 1. Diversity among religions and religious communities is obvious. But only in recent decades have most Western Christians come into direct, personal contact with people of other religious traditions. What are we to make of these "others"? Do we ignore them? Persecute them? Try to "persuade" them that they are wrong? Christians have at times related to non-Christians in all these ways. In Europe and North America, the numbers of Christians and individual congregations are declining. In Africa, Asia, and parts of South America, however, large numbers of people are becoming "Christian." This increase in numbers is in many instances taking place in parts of the world where Islam is also rapidly growing. Conflicts are taking place now, and more are quite likely unless we can find a way theologically to understand the "others" without making them "our enemies" or the "enemies of God." The issue must be addressed at the individual level as well as the community level. Such concerns will be explored in chapters 1 and 2.

Methodology is not often very interesting to nonspecialists, but it is important to give some indication of how the Bible is being studied and interpreted in light of new findings that will be claimed. While we will not spend an undue amount of time on this topic, some explication is necessary. Contextual interpretation is most needed. This involves a careful study of the biblical passages in question. It also requires an engagement with the contemporary, multicultural communities in which most of us live. Chapter 3 will be devoted to this important matter.

The Bible in itself is composed of a wide variety of diverse materials and viewpoints. There are many valid ways to consider who God is and what God is up to. In light of the picture drawn in part 1, questions concerning the "truthfulness" of non-Christian religions are important for many contemporary Christians. For centuries the church has taught that faith in Christ was the only way to relationship with God. But is that what the Bible teaches? Important questions need to be raised about prior teaching by the church on this matter. Some key passages in the Bible need to be reconsidered. In light of what the Bible has to say, is there a better approach? This will be the focus of part 2. Chapters 4 through 8 will be devoted to this exploration.

Finally, in part 3, attention will turn to what may be some of the next practical steps that might be taken so that my mother's question need not continue to haunt me/us. What has been done to better understand other religions? What kinds of cross-cultural and interfaith exchanges have been helpful? Particularly with respect to Islam, how do we overcome the deep-seated suspicions and ignorance among many Christians and Muslims concerning one another? Already Christianity and Islam respectively are the number-one and number-two religions in the world so far as numbers go. How can mutual understanding and cooperation be fostered? Or is destructive, divisive confrontation the future for Christians and Muslims? What is to be learned from interaction with other religions as well? Chapters 9 through 12 will take up these questions.

The Aim of This Study

In summary, this book to some extent intends to explore the religious diversity in our world with open eyes and listening hearts. It is hoped that a reconsideration of some key biblical passages will assist in a reorientation that I think is crucial for the church to make. Finally, some concrete suggestions for engagement with others will be offered. The desired outcome is encouragement to listen to all the "mothers" in our congregations who are asking some simple, straightforward questions about the content and meaning of our precious Bible and who deserve honest responses to their concerns.

PART 1

A New Context

Opening Our Eyes

Chapter 1

A New Game

Some years ago the reality of diversity hit me squarely in the eyes and ears. I was in New York City and had to transfer from one airline to another. I took a shortcut and walked across the parking lot reserved for taxicabs servicing Manhattan's LaGuardia Airport. In that short five-minute walk from one terminal building to another, I encountered a new world, at least to me. There was an array of people who spoke at least thirty different languages, with English as a very second—sometimes fourth or fifth—language for almost all of them. This group of cab drivers, consisting of people from who-knows-how-many lands and ethnic backgrounds, each with their own distinctive clothing, hairstyles, and so forth, was milling about waiting for the next fare. Such an experience can be mind-boggling—and sometimes unnerving—particularly for those of us from the hinterland who do not regularly encounter such difference and diversity in large numbers "up close and personal." It certainly was for me.

To be sure, New York City is atypical. It is not like most other places in the United States. Nonetheless, with New York City we see a microcosm of our world. What we see there gives us a glimpse of the diverse context in which we live. In 2001, for instance, the schoolchildren of New York City actually spoke some 140 languages when they began their educations. For a large number of them, English was new. Of its some 8.2 million inhabitants, approximately 37 percent, well over 3 million, are first- or second-generation immigrants. New York City has unarguably the largest and most diverse population in the United States. At least 170 languages are reported to be spoken there. That is surely extraordinary to most of us. But in fact that represents only a small portion of the world's estimated 6,912 different tongues! If one wants to begin to understand the potentials and problems that the diverse character of our world presents, New York City provides an excellent place to start.

And what about religion in this diverse world of ours? In New York City, based on the 2000 census, about 40% are Catholics, 30% Protestants, 13% claiming no religious affiliation, 5% Jews, 3.5% Muslims, and 1% Buddhists. In terms of the estimated numbers worldwide, the picture looks somewhat different. Worldwide there are approximately 2.1 billion Christians, 1.3 billion Muslims, 1.1 billion secularists, 900 million Hindus, 394 million Chinese traditional religionists, 376 million Buddhists, 14 million Jews, and 179 million members of other smaller religious communities.

Some years ago Diana Eck of Harvard University, who has done incredible work in mapping the religious landscape of the United States in the past fifteen years, interpreted the worldwide data in a way that made things easier for me to comprehend. She wrote:

> If our world were a village of a thousand people, who would *we* be? The World Development Forum tells us that there would be 329 Christians, 174 Muslims, 131 Hindus, 61 Buddhists, 52 Animists, 3 Jews, 34 members of other religions, such as Sikhs, Jains, Zoroastrians, and Baha'is, and 216 would be without any religion. In this village, there would be 564 Asians, 210 Europeans, 86 Africans, 80 South Americans, and 60 North Americans. And in this same village 60 persons would have half the income, 500 would be hungry, 600 would live in shantytowns, and 700 would be illiterate. (Eck 1993, 202)

In considering the worldwide figures, while they are only estimates, several things should be noted. First, the term "Christian" includes *all* those who claim the title (Catholics, Protestants, Pentecostals, Evangelicals, Eastern Orthodox, Anglicans, Monophysites, Latter-day Saints [Mormons], Seventh-day Adventists, Jehovah's Witnesses, Quakers, some indigenous African "new" religions, etc.). The largest groups within the "Christian" category are Catholics and Pentecostals. Further, not all those designated "Christian" would agree that all others belong. Second, the actual population figures among the Christians of Asia, Africa, and South America, in comparison to Europe and North America, are growing dramatically. Already the preponderance of Christians live in the Southern Hemisphere, not the Northern Hemisphere, as we in the United States have so long taken for granted. Thus, the view of the "world"—particularly the religious "world"—as many North Americans experience it, except in places like New York City and perhaps Chicago and Los Angeles, is skewed. Third, the largest increases in religious affiliation are among Christians (mainly Roman Catholics and Pentecostals, not the mainline Protestant churches) and among Muslims (mainly Sunni, though the Shiites get more attention in the press these days). Indeed, it has recently been reported in the press that, worldwide, Muslims now outnumber the Roman Catholics, the largest single Christian group.

Whether we like it or not, however, we increasingly find ourselves, in this country in the twenty-first century, in a unique situation. The United States is now the most religiously diverse country in the world. While still predominantly "Christian," other groups are growing steadily. This is well documented by Professor Eck, who with the help of numerous others has gathered the evidence of the extraordinary proliferation of religious communities across the United States that has occurred in the past twenty-five or thirty years (2001).

Immigration has clearly been a factor in the emergence of significant non-Christian communities in the United States, but so has "conversion." Many of those with no religion and some, perhaps born into Christian families but not engaged by their churches, have joined non-Christian groups. Now, "they," who believe differently than "we," are no longer on the other side of the world. "They" live across the street. "They" work alongside us. "They" send their children to the same schools that "we" do, struggle with dress codes, and wonder what it means when public officials (and others) insist that this is a "Christian" nation. Indeed, "they," like us, do all the things that citizens do.

And guess what? My personal context, and I suspect yours as well, has changed! I mean really changed! Political, economic, sociological, ethnic diversity is now the *rule* rather than the *exception,* right where I live. This is very important to recognize and important to appropriate into my efforts to understand and interpret the Bible, and anything else for that matter. The world is considerably smaller, metaphorically speaking, than it was at the time of my birth. In the religious sphere, for instance, when I was growing up, "others" in my part of the world consisted mainly of Baptists, Methodists, Church of Christ, a few Pentecostals, and the Roman Catholics, who were mysteriously different from all the rest. (Of course, as a Presbyterian I was actually one of the "others," but I didn't know it!) As one who is theologically aware, I have to acknowledge and account for this diversity.

Where I now reside, in a city in the Midwest with a population of just under a million, I live as neighbor to Jews, Muslims, Buddhists, Baha'is, Hindus, New Age believers, a large variety of Christians, and many other people who consider themselves spiritually sensitive and aware, though they do not belong to any organized religion. And of course, there is a very large group of neofundamentalists—to be encountered, by the way, in almost every religious tradition—who regularly express their conviction, if not their desire, that all the rest of us "others" will spend eternity in a rather uncomfortable place.

My/our situation has indeed changed. It may not be as radically different as that of a newly arrived immigrant or someone who has for generations been "left out" because of prejudice and oppression. But it is different, and requires me/us to recognize how it is different. Perhaps must obvious, I can no longer automatically operate—on the basis of social privilege—as part of the "establishment." As a Presbyterian I am clearly part of a distinct minority. In fact, as a member of the so-called mainline churches, I am in a group that is losing influence and social "power" daily.

Worldwide, Christians still constitute the largest religious group, but we are divided into so many subgroups that we certainly can't act as one on any matter of significance. As in the first century (as we will consider later), diversity among Christians and among religions is the norm, not the exception. And I belong to a minority, not a majority, at least as far as the wider world is concerned. All too often Christians have taken Jesus' teaching about being present where two or three are gathered in his name (Matthew 18:20) one step further than was probably intended, to mean that each such "group" should start a new denomination. In my own tradition there are more than two hundred separate churches/denominations that call themselves "Reformed" and belong to the World Alliance of Reformed Churches. So much for Christian unity!

The point of all this is that diversity, within the church and with the many other religions in the world, is now a fact of our existence, whether we fully recognize it yet or not. As Christians, sooner or later, we are going to have to deal with it. We can continue with the traditional exclusivist approach that considers all other expressions of religion outside our own to be wrong. Or we may take a more open, inclusive position that allows that while we consider our approach "best," we nonetheless acknowledge that others do have some measure of "truth" in their religions. Or, with some, we might adopt an even more "radical" view, a pluralist position, and consider all religions of value and all religious people as those from whom we might have something to learn. In *The Wide, Wide Circle of Divine Love* (2005) I explored these options and came down somewhere between the second and third. That discussion will continue in this volume because it remains a critical issue.

In his book *The World Is Flat,* Thomas L. Friedman wrote about two context-changing events for those in the United States and the wider world as well. On November 11, 1989—11/9 in Friedman's symbolic shorthand—the fall of the Berlin Wall occurred, a very positive event from Friedman's point of view and that of the West in general. And on September 11, 2001—9/11—the fall of the Twin Towers in New York City was broadcast by live TV around the world, clearly a very negative event, which shattered public confidence in many places. Friedman used these events metaphorically to reflect on the role of imagination in dealing with the new economic and trade realities he saw emerging:

> There are two ways to flatten the world. One is to use your imagination to bring everyone up to the same level, and the other is to use your imagination to bring everyone down to the same level. (2005, 447)
>
> Those of us who are fortunate to live in free and progressive societies have to set an example. We have to be the best global citizens we can be. We cannot retreat from the world. We have to make sure that we get the best of our own imaginations—and never let our imaginations get the best of us. (448)

He then turned more specifically to religious imagination:

> Religions are the smelters and founders of imagination. The more any religion's imagination—Hindu, Christian, Jewish, Muslim,

Buddhist—is shaped in an isolated bubble, or in a dark cave, the more its imagination is likely to sail off in dangerous directions. People who are connected to the world and exposed to different cultures and perspectives are far more likely to develop the imagination of 11/9. People who are feeling disconnected, for whom personal freedom and fulfillment are a utopian fantasy, are more likely to develop the imagination of 9/11.

Friedman was in no way suggesting that the difficulties of dealing with people and cultures radically different from our own are imaginary. Rather, he was challenging those of us in places of leadership to make positive use of our imaginations in finding appropriate and useful ways of helping our people understand and adapt to the new diversity that is changing our world, both internationally and locally. Religiously as well as economically speaking, the world is becoming "flat." "Pluralism" is not just a "politically correct" term. It is a reality that we must learn to deal with economically, sociologically, and theologically. And if history repeats itself, our theological struggle may well be more difficult and more divisive than our economic and sociological ones.

Once again we reflect on the work of Diana Eck:

The story of the new religious America is an unfinished story, with both national and global implications. The chapters of the story are still being written in cities and towns all over the country. Whether the vibrant new religious diversity that is now part and parcel of the United States, will, in the years ahead, bring us together or tear us apart depends greatly on whether we are able to imagine our national community anew. And the fate of a vibrant pluralism in the U.S. will have an important impact on the fate of religious pluralism worldwide. The ongoing argument over who "we" are—as religious people, as a nation, and as a global community—is one in which all of us, ready or not, will participate. (2001, 385)

Yes, who we are as a religious people is very much up for grabs. If we are to move beyond the current status quo, two things are critical. First, we will need to revisit our foundational document, the Bible, in the light of our new context. With open eyes and minds we need to reconsider if and how the Bible can help us as we approach the issues of diversity and pluralism. The religious diversity so pre-valent in the first centuries of our tradition, a topic we will consider in the next chapter, has much to teach us. We will do well to explore different interpretative methods and consider alternative understand-ings of passages we have long treasured. Sometimes this will mean unlearning what we have been long taught. At other times (and prob-ably more often!) it will mean learning what we never knew. The reconsideration of cherished traditions is never easy, but it seems more and more an imperative if we are to respond faithfully in our new situation.

A second issue is equally critical. We must find the will and the medium by which to educate our people about our new historical con-text. We may be able to find a new approach to the Bible and to the-ology, but unless we can communicate the results to our people effectively, not much can change positively. The upheavals of the changing landscape of our world are upon us, and so also is our expe-rience of the contemporary religious diversity that is increasing so dramatically within our communities. We have too often been reluc-tant to talk with one another about our own personal experience of God for fear of sounding "weird" or "religious," but the varieties of our experience as Christians among Christians and as compared with others who are not Christian are important to consider.

Changes are taking place. The issue is how we will respond. Will we turn them for the good of our communities or not? Can we help-fully respond to the questions my mom posed or not? We really won't know until we try. One verse from Psalms is worth remembering as we proceed:

> All the ends of the earth shall remember and turn to the LORD;
> And all the families of the nations shall worship before him.
> (Psalm 22:27)

Discussion Questions

1. What is the character and extent of religious diversity where you live? How does that compare/contrast with the diversity described in this chapter?

2. According to Thomas Friedman it is critical that religious leaders constructively use their imaginations to refashion the religious interpretation of life for the twenty-first century. Why? What are some of the possibilities?
3. Why (according to Diana Eck) is it important to struggle with the "vibrant pluralism" that is gaining expression in the United States? What are some of the ways this might begin?

Chapter 2

The Diversity Matrix

*M*y mother wanted to know, "When did they put that in there?" Just as those verses from Isaiah startled my mom, so the Bible continues to surprise people. There is so much in it that is essentially unknown so far as the general public is concerned. And what is known usually consists of a relatively small number of passages or verses entirely removed from their literary and historical contexts.

Now the fact is, of course, that the Bible has not changed much since it was first written, but our (trained biblical scholars') knowledge of the Bible, and the context in which we now read it, has changed dramatically! The numerous new translations of the Bible and the continuing production of new commentaries to assist with the study of the Bible give testimony to the explosion of knowledge that has taken place in the past fifty years. From the treasure trove of thousands of cuneiform tablets recovered at the site of the ancient city Ebla in Syria to the most recent public eye-catcher, the *Gospel of Judas,* new data from the ancient world are producing scholarly and popular reappraisal of long-held opinions. Greater understanding of the ancient languages, clearer insight into the social customs of the day, and a more accurate history of the societies of antiquity are emerging; with this new information comes the need for new interpretation, for reformulation. To make sense of all this theologically compels us to consider the Bible anew.

We need to reengage our tradition, but this is difficult. We have understood the Bible from our "old" point of view for so long. How can we jump-start our religious imaginations and move in a new direction? How can we open ourselves for a fresh encounter with our foundational document, the Bible? There is never going to be any foolproof method by which to listen to the biblical message or to discern God's hand in our lives. And to be sure, the assistance of the Holy Spirit is essential. Nonetheless, in the past thirty years or so there has emerged an approach to interpretation that is worth considering, an approach that might help us get off dead center. It is called "contextual interpretation."

Thus far contextual interpretation has been mainly associated with what some would call "special-interest" groups. I prefer to call these groups, and their interpreters, "special awareness" groups. They consist of folk who have been, or are, marginalized, so far as the mainstream is concerned, by reason of sex, race, ethnic background, or what have you. These groups constitute minorities, and their interpreters address their minorities from a position that is "outside" the majority cultures in which they live.

Black theologians, feminist theologians, and liberation theologians have led the way. More recently, members of various ethnic groups—Korean, Native American, and Latinos of various backgrounds—have accepted the challenge as well. By reflecting on their own particular social location, they have heard old texts differently with a fresh urgency and a more immediate relevance. One African American interpreter has suggested, for instance, that Joseph and Mary "found no place in the inn" on that first Christmas morning because they were the target, in effect, of "Jim Crow laws" aimed at Galileans.

These contextual interpreters have teased out the socioeconomic implications of the biblical text for their own particular groups and situations. They have not tried to claim universal applicability for their insights. Rather, they rightly insist on the correctness of their understandings for *their* circumstances. They read the Bible from within their own particular contexts and try to make sense of what is being said *for them* considering *who* they are, *where* they are, and *what* they actually can and should do. As I have said, the term "contextual interpretation" has been given to their approach.

Now, trained theologians and informed readers in general know how important context is in considering a biblical text, or anything else for that matter. In trying to understand what a biblical passage may mean, the literary context is obviously the most basic context to explore. Where does the passage appear? How is it shaped rhetorically? How does it interact with its context? How does the text fit in with respect to the vocabulary and style of its immediate and wider literary context? Is a typical literary type or form employed? How does the literary character of the text aid or hinder interpretation? What is the historical context of the passage, both in terms of the literary setting and in terms of when the text was probably written? These questions have long been basic to the literary/historical approach that most contemporary North American and European biblical scholars employ. They are important questions and not to be ignored.

More recently, however, as already noted, those who have pioneered contextual interpretation have added a new and very important dimension to the task: the careful analysis of their own, contemporary contexts. What are the particular social and economic realities of first-generation immigrants to the United States, for instance? What special situations confront persons in minority groups? How can the Bible address the real needs of these persons? Contextual interpretation takes the consideration of such questions very seriously and tries thereby to open the eyes and hearts of their audience to a fresh understanding of the implications of biblical texts for such special and particular circumstances.

Whether one belongs to one of the special awareness groups or not, one can, with effort, participate in the disciplined interpretative process championed by contextual interpreters. Most of us are accustomed to asking the literary/historical questions, informally if not always formally. Now we need to reflect with equal care on our present social circumstance. Whether we are aware of it or not, a number of things have changed or are changing in our society and in the church. This analysis is not easily done since we are in the midst of our current circumstances. It is difficult to gain perspective from within a situation. Nonetheless that is our task.

At least two major factors should inform our reading of the Bible. First, there is the wealth of new information about the diversity that marked the early centuries of the Christian movement. Second, there is a major realignment taking place within the Christian world, a major redistribution of the Christian population. This will be news for many North Americans, less so for Europeans. Whatever one's reaction, one's reading and interpretation of the Bible will be affected. We will devote the rest of this chapter to the first concern, the diversity matrix, and the next chapter to the new status of North American and European Christians on the world stage.

So, let us turn to a review of the beginnings of our tradition, the very diverse matrix from which the Christian movement emerged. Though it has long been assumed otherwise by many, diversity rather than unity prevailed in the early church. Through new research and new data, we have come to a much greater knowledge of the societies from which Judaism and Christianity emerged. The Roman Empire was marked by a high degree of ethnic and religious diversity.

Only toward the middle of the second century CE, more than a century after the life, death, and resurrection of Jesus, did some uniformity, at least in practice, begin to take shape. Even then, however, many differences in experience and interpretation continued among and between Christians. The same was true of Jewish communities as well. By then, the separation between Jews and Christians, which had been minimal in the beginning, was increasing as well with each new generation.

By the end of the second century CE, two new religions had emerged, the religions we now name "Christianity" and "Judaism," parallel in many ways but clearly distinct. Before the middle of the second century it is technically incorrect to talk about either "Christians" or "Jews," though of course we do. But we need to remind ourselves that this practice is anachronistic, obscuring the gradual emergence and separation of both religions from one another.

To try to bring greater precision to our thinking about this early period, some scholars are avoiding the use of the terms "Christian" or "Jew" in describing the people of the era, particularly in the first century and a half of the Common Era. The "Christians" were in the beginning mainly "Jews" who followed the Galilean rabbi Jesus. The "Jews," at least in the New Testament, were people who lived mainly in the Roman province of Judea. Caroline Johnson Hodge puts it this way:

> I prefer *Ioudaioi* [Judeans] for two linked reasons. First, I want to avoid the term "Jew," which in the modern world can evoke a concept of a religious identity separate from an ethnic. In the ancient Mediterranean cultures, religious identity and ethnic identity were interrelated and mutually constituting. The term "Jew," because of its modern associations, can mask this relationship.

Second, I use "Judean" in order to maintain the parallels inherent in the Greek with other ethnic designations such as "Greek," "Egyptian," "Roman," and so on. (Zangenberg and Labahn 2004, 79)

During this same time the Hebrew Bible was being fashioned. Before the early decades of the second century of the Common Era, there was no official "Bible" for either the Judeans or the followers of Jesus. Tradition had elevated the Torah (the first five books of the Bible that Christians today sometimes call the Pentateuch) and the Prophets (known among Christians today as the books of Joshua–Kings, Isaiah, Jeremiah, Ezekiel, and the twelve Minor Prophets), but there was no fixed agreement about all the other books we now find in the Bible. A group of Judeans of the Pharisaic Party were those who finally put together the list of books, the canon, which now serves as the Hebrew Bible.

Though we like to simplify historical matters, the development of the Hebrew Bible was not easy or clear-cut. There were thriving, diverse communities of "Jews" in Egypt and Babylonia, and elsewhere around the Mediterranean basin, which gave diversity and vitality to the Judaism which was emerging. There was a debate about which books should become part of the Hebrew Bible, what writings should constitute the "canon."

Because the Romans had destroyed Jerusalem, first in 70 CE and again in 135 CE, there was perhaps less religious diversity among "Jews" in Palestine than anywhere else in the Roman Empire. The Romans had expelled most of the "Jews," the Judeans (so far as the Romans were concerned, this term included those who came to be called "Christian" as well), from Jerusalem and Judea. A small number of Judeans of the Pharisaic Party were allowed to form a school at Jamnia (Jabne), a coastal town about fifteen or twenty miles south of modern-day Tel Aviv. It was this group that produced the Palestinian version of the "canon" that won final endorsement. To gain acceptance by the war-weary Judeans, some of the more "radical" literature (e.g., apocalyptic material that was considered anti-Rome) was omitted. Nonetheless, the Bible that was authorized provided plenty of contrasting materials to support a wide variety of positions.

During this same time, the Judean and Galilean followers of Jesus, at least those who understood Hebrew, used this canon as their Bible.

Greek-speaking Christians, however, used another, slightly larger, and somewhat different version of the Bible known now as the Septuagint, which had originated in Egypt. Eventually (1,500 years later) Protestant Christians chose the Hebrew Bible as their Old Testament while Orthodox Christians and Roman Catholics settled on the Septuagint and/or its Latin translation, the Vulgate. Some of our ongoing theological debates arise because of the difference in the basic shape of the Bibles we choose to study.

It is important to remember that at the very time when the books that we call the New Testament were being written, Christians were a distinct minority, first among Jews, and even more so within Roman society at large. They were outsiders. They read some version of the Bible (either in Hebrew or Greek). There was no theological standard by which to sort out "heresy" from "orthodoxy." The "canon" of the New Testament (the list of the agreed-upon contents) was not finally arrived at until the fifth century CE. Many different and sometimes competing groups of Christians existed. The *Gospel of Peter* and the *Gospel of Judas* no doubt reflected the beliefs of different groups of Christians, just as did the Gospels of Mark and John.

In commenting upon the circumstances of the early centuries of the Christian movement in Rome, Peter Lampe has written:

> Early Christians in Rome formed various house churches. These groups met in private homes. There was no local center for Roman Christianity. This factionalism, similar to that of the Jews in the city, facilitated a theological pluralism. Thus, second-century Rome saw Christian groups following numerous theological directions: Marcionite, Valentinian, Carpocratian, Theodotian, Modalistic, Montanist and Quartodecimanian teachings. There were Cerdo's followers and house churches of (what was only later called) the "orthodox" faith. There existed a Jewish-Christian circle that still observed the Torah. . . . Some groups exhibited a logos theology that was too complicated for lesser educated Christians. Some circles believed in the millennium and others did not. Roman Christianity was multicoloured and as such often also reflected the various geographical and educational provenances of Roman Christians. (Zangenberg and Labahn 2004, 26)

Reading anew the texts that were written in this historical era in light of this new understanding may perhaps help us deal with our new status and new situation as one group among many others in a very religiously diverse world. Diversity was the norm, not the exception, and both Jews and Christians flourished.

What's more, the constituencies of each group knew that they lived as distinct minorities within the Roman Empire. They had no illusions of power. Their texts were written within their own communities primarily for their own people. They were accordingly "contextually interpreted." Even when Christians and Jews addressed or accused one another, they did so as members of one minority to another, neither of which had any real power to do much more than challenge or harass the other. The highly diverse context of the early centuries of the Christian movement is critically important for contemporary Christians to remember. We were not in the majority at the beginning. Rather, at the outset Christians were a powerless minority—let me repeat: a powerless minority!

It was not until the fourth century, under Emperor Constantine, in 324 CE, that Christianity as a religion became established. With the legalization of the Christian church and then the designation of Christianity as the official religion of the empire, enormous changes came in social and political circumstances for Christians (e.g., Carroll 2001, 67–236). There was a clear redistribution of power and, predictably, changes in the interpretation of the Bible took place. Christians were no longer a powerless minority. They were now among the ruling majority. While not in keeping with most of the foundational documents preserved in the New Testament (the Second Testament), a claim of religious superiority began to emerge. This new replacement theology, now called supersessionism, became the recognized interpretation.

The basic contention of this theology was that the Christian church had replaced Israel as the people of God. As the "chosen people," Christians, then, were "better" than all other peoples. Conversion or death was the option that many Christians assumed appropriate for all non-Christians. For centuries this teaching went largely unchallenged and has, in my opinion, led Christians astray. Now in the twenty-first century the "truth" of this position has come under critical scrutiny and is being strongly challenged. The way for a fresh appraisal of our texts is slowly but steadily opening, and none too soon.

Our new context suggests that we reconsider our basic theological assumptions by listening again to the foundational texts, particularly the Bible. Is the exclusivist we-against-them reading that has so long prevailed in the church a necessary logical consequence of super-sessionism? If so, is that the only or the best way to read the Bible faithfully? Is there any positive word for a time such as ours, a word that is inclusive rather than exclusive, a word that will challenge me to be a good neighbor and not a disdainful, dismissive, arrogant one? A careful analysis of the contexts, then and now, is one way perhaps to uncover these needed gracious words. The insights gained by those who have pioneered contextual interpretation may be most useful.

We are certainly living in a time when hostility within and between some religious communities seems to be intensifying. Name-calling, stereotyping, profiling, exclusivism, fear of the foreigner and the stranger, all justified in the name of religion, are readily apparent wherever one looks. Toleration is sadly missing. But in fact we need more than what we commonly understand as tolerance. We need a positive appropriation of the diversity, the pluralism, which is now our context. Michael Jinkins has expressed well the challenge before us:

> But what would it mean to account for religious diversity within a pluralistic framework? . . . This would require resisting the temp-tation to make absolute claims, either on behalf of an ideal, trans-historical set of criteria beyond all religions, or of making our own faith claims absolute. And it would mean resisting the perhaps even more subtle temptation to make judgements on the relative value and trustworthiness of religious faiths from a superior position out-side human histories and cultures. (2004, 113–14)
>
> This quality of pluralism, "real pluralism" (objective pluralism) practiced by "real" Christians (confessing, practicing Christians who refuse to submit their faith to reductionism), again, is made possible if we do not believe that our faith in God grants us a priv-ileged position outside of the particularity of our own faith, some-how above history, culture, and all religions, which allows us to pronounce judgement on the relative truthfulness of one religion over another. (115)

I share the sentiments of Jinkins. I see divine providence in the great variety of the religions in the world. The richness of religious devotion is enhanced as one recognizes that religious diversity is not an enemy but a guide. God's way of love has provided a rich tapestry for us to study and experience, and in so doing to recognize our special place in God's beautiful work. But we must have open, reality-perceiving eyes and a listening, compassionate heart if we are to see God's amazing deeds.

Discussion Questions

1. What is meant by "contextual interpretation" in this chapter? How do the wealth of new information now available and the redistribution of the Christian population affect our "context"?
2. How did Christianity and Judaism emerge in parallel in the Roman world of the second century? What are some of the implications of sharing an emerging body of writing that has come to be called the Bible?
3. What impact did the fact of being small minorities in their religiously plural world have on Christians and Jews alike? How did the "success" of Constantine alter the situation? Was it for the better or the worse?

Chapter 3

No Longer Number One

*T*he chant: "We're number one! We're number one!" has migrated in the United States from the sport field to any number of other venues. Americans seem captivated by the question "Who's number one?" Is it my business? My community? My church? My country? Even little children go around with their fingers high in the air, claiming the number-one status for one thing or another. Americans like to be number one. Thus it comes as a shock to many that, while Christianity as a world religion can still boast of having the largest number of adherents, North America and Europe cannot make a similar claim. We in North America and Europe, so far as the numbers of Christians in our midst are concerned, are no longer number one!

Along with the new awareness of the great diversity in our religious world now and during the inaugural centuries of both Judaism and Christianity, another change in our situation has occurred. For a long time, for at least three centuries if not more, European and North American Christians constituted the vast majority of the world's Christian population. They/we occupied the positions of power and influence. They/we were the backbone—indeed, the body—for most of the communities in which we lived. They/we supplied financial support and leadership assistance all around the world. From hospitals to orphanages, from agricultural training to theological training, they/we provided so much for the "younger churches." They/we have been "exporters" of religion as well as many other kinds of support. But a fundamental change is under way.

The center of the Christian world is no longer located in North America and Europe. Since 1900 the Christian population of Africa has grown from an estimated 9 million to some 380 million in 2000. In 1900 about 80 percent of the Christians in the world lived in Europe and North America. In 2000 some 60 percent of the Christians lived in the global South or East (Sanneh and Carpenter 2005). The Roman Catholic Church constitutes the largest Christian body in the world (somewhat over a billion adherents). Roman Catholics also constitute the largest Christian group in the United States. But fewer than a tenth of the Catholics worldwide live in the United States. So far as other Christian groups are concerned (almost another billion adherents), there are approximately three times as many who live outside North America as within it.

In some places shifts in numbers have come because of the conversion of people to Christianity (particularly in sub-Saharan Africa) or because of immigration of Christians from one country into another (as with Asian and Hispanic Roman Catholics into the United States). In some places the increase or decrease is associated more directly with the overall population growth or decline of an area. The size of families among North American and European Christians, for instance, has tended to become smaller; fewer children are being born. At the same time the number of children in Christian families elsewhere around the globe has increased. Demographics tell the story, and a visit to the numerous empty or nearly empty churches scattered across the countryside will confirm them. The bottom line is clear: so far as the United States and Europe are concerned, significant decreases in the number of adherents have occurred. In the world's South and East, however, there have been dramatic increases.

What's more, Christians outside North America and Europe are now doing their own theology, no longer "importing" it from us as in the past. The African Initiated Churches (or the African Independent Churches), for instance, are developing their own, quite distinctive theology and rituals. Stephen B. Bevans comments:

> How can the important symbol of baptism express cleansing and inclusion when, in the Masai culture of Africa, pouring water over a woman's head is a ritual cursing her to barrenness? Christianity's insistence on monogamy and condemnation of polygamy ignores an important structure for women's security in African societies where women outnumber men and kinship patterns and obligations differ significantly from those of Europe. (1992, 5–6)

The interpretation of Christianity and the Bible that has been "normative" for the past several hundred years—namely, a European and North American version of that "truth"—is being challenged and recast. Added to the two classical loci for theological reflection (Scripture and tradition) is personal experience; and African, Central and South American, and Asian Christian life experience is often quite different from that of most North American and European Christians (Bevans 1992, 1–2).

This reinterpretation or contextualizing is not necessarily bad, but it is different. It does require that Christians in North America and Europe reconsider some assumptions and, as necessary, learn how to listen to other voices coming with other experiences from other places. We must develop a new way of seeing and a deeper level of empathy and understanding in our hearts. This is not easy, and it cannot be done alone.

Walter Dietrich and Ulrich Luz have edited an interesting set of essays and reflections by Christians from several social settings outside North America and Europe, titled *The Bible in a World Context.* Elsa Tamez, a noted Christian leader in Costa Rica, contributed a provocative essay, "Reading the Bible under a Sky without Stars." In it she reflects on the inadequacies of language, particularly when trying to translate from one language to another. She pondered how to "explain" the meaning of the Spanish word often translated as "abundance." She introduced her reflections with the following story about a Mayan sage. Canek, the Mayan sage, said to Guy, a fragile and noble child of the plantation:

> "Look at the sky; count the stars."
> "It is not possible to count them."

Canek spoke to him again:

> "Look at the earth; count the grains of sand."
> "It is not possible to count them."

Canek then said:

> "Even though it is not known, there exists a number for the stars and a number for the grains of sand. But that which exists and cannot be counted and is felt herewith requires a word to say it. The

word in this case would be 'abundance.' It is a word moist with mystery. This word makes it unnecessary to count the stars or the grains of sand. We have traded *knowledge* for *emotion,* which is also a way to penetrate into the truth of things." (Tamez 2002, 3)

"Moist with mystery!" To lapse into such poetic expression is to "trade *knowledge* for *emotion.*" This is not the usual way we in North America go about the interpretative task. To many it will seem strange, but if we are to interact with our Christian sisters and brothers around the world—especially since they now constitute the majority—we need to consider changing some of our ways of doing things. Listening hearts is what we need.

Interpreters such as Tamez are suggesting that we ponder the mysteries of the faith without insisting on quantifying everything. The disastrous effects that colonialism and imperialism have worked in Latin America, all too often in the name of Christianity, cannot be expressed only in the language of quantifiable knowledge. The disaster must be felt! And that is in the realm of emotion. New interpretation prompted by, and true to, lived reality is called for. Such interpretation is being brought forth, but North American and European Christians no longer dominate or control this process. (See also three other studies devoted to sample exploration of important contextual theologies: for Asia, Chung, Kärkkäinen, and Kyoung-Jae 2007; for India, Wilfred 1995; for Latin America, Aponte and De La Torre 2006.)

Related to the shift in the Christian population center is another change in our reality that we need to recognize clearly, with eyes wide open, and then we must address it. Philip Jenkins points to an enormous challenge on the very near horizon.

At the turn of the third millennium, religious loyalties are at the root of many of the world's ongoing civil wars and political violence, and in most cases, the critical division is the age-old battle between Christianity and Islam. However much this would have surprised political analysts a generation or two ago, the critical political frontiers around the world are not decided by attitudes toward class or dialectical materialism, but by rival concepts of God. (Jenkins 2002, 161)

Demographic projections suggest that religious feuds will not only continue but will also become worse. The future centers of global population are chiefly in countries that are already divided between the two great religions, and where divisions are likely to intensify. In present-day battles in Africa and Asia, we may today be seeing the political outlines of the new century, and probably, the roots of future great power alliances. (162)

Since the horrifying events of 9/11, the citizens of the United States have become painfully aware of a Muslim world that had, in many respects, been ignored (or perhaps at least tolerated because of the oil the West wants to fuel our enormous consumer appetite). In the wake of the suicide attacks, the preemptive attacks on Afghanistan and Iraq, and the increasing xenophobia (particularly provoked by anyone who looks Middle Eastern and also more recently by Hispanics who are also considered in the United States as a threat to "our way of life"), the need to encourage and enable understanding between Christians and those of other faiths, particularly Islam, is reaching the crisis stage.

This is true for the United States. It is even more critical in France and England, where there is presently a much greater concentration of Muslims. But the real battlegrounds are going to be in places like Nigeria, Indonesia, and the Philippines, where large Muslim communities live in close proximity or in the midst of equally large Christian communities and where the constraints of democratic institutions and traditions do not prevail. We as the "forebears," if no longer the "directors," of our Christian brothers and sisters around the world have a responsibility to do some serious thinking about how we are all to live in this world of such enormous religious diversity.

We cannot determine what others think about us, but we can and should be clear about how we think about others. The approach of the colonial powers (and here I include the United States) to the peoples of the third world was for a long time condescending at best. We assumed that our culture was in every way better, and we did our best to impose it on the others. This included "our" religion, Christianity. Now I in no way want to cease in sharing the good news I know in Jesus Christ, but we need to develop better ways of doing that sharing. It is quite important whether we consider other human beings to have been created "in the image of God" (e.g., Genesis 1:26–27) or not. Rather than the disdainful approach that has marked so much of

Christian theological reflection about other religions for so long, we need a new understanding, a new definition of the relationship of Christianity to the other religions of the world. Does God actually love other people like God loves us?

One additional aspect of our new situation should be noted. My/our situation may not be as radically different as that of a newly arrived immigrant or someone who has for generations been left out because of prejudice and oppression, but it is different. That difference requires me/us to recognize just how it is different. As noted previously, those in the mainline Christian denominations have for a long time constituted, in essence, the establishment. Technically, of course, no religion is the official religion in the United States. But that has not stopped many people from acting otherwise. Now, however, with the changes in circumstance that are more and more obvious to all, such is becoming less and less possible. In my case, for instance, even if all the Presbyterians were united (and they are not!), we still would be a distinct minority within what is already part of the Protestant minority within the worldwide Christian movement. Indeed, there are considerably more Pentecostals in the United States now than there are Presbyterians!

Worldwide, Christians may still constitute the largest religious group in terms of gross membership numbers, but we are divided into so many subgroups that we certainly can't act as one on any matter of significance. As in the first century, diversity among Christians is the norm, not the exception. What's more, Christians are now more clearly than ever seeking to demonstrate God's love in a world where there is competition. We do not have a monopoly on God or on divine love. Adherents of other religions that are significant and vibrant are at work as well. Islam claims over a billion constituents and is growing more rapidly than Christianity in many parts of the world. This presents a challenge indeed to all who long for an end to religious wars and all other disruptions of peace and wholeness in our world. We need not discount the efforts of others to proclaim the love of God, but to celebrate such efforts requires of us a change of understanding, a heart renovation.

The contextual interpreters, whom we have mentioned above, have rightly sensed that we now need to try to hear the Bible anew in light of the circumstances of our own particular groups and situations. There may eventually be a place for applying what we learn in a more universal fashion, but that is not our first responsibility. Rather, we need to read the Bible from within our own particular contexts, in this new situation in which we find ourselves. We need to try to make sense of what is being said in the ancient texts that is pertinent *for us now* considering *who* we are, *where* we are, and *what* we actually can and should do.

Among other things already noted, this means that we read as members of a minority in the midst of a religiously pluralistic and diverse world! Our "power" resides almost exclusively in our ability to persuade and to demonstrate by our lifestyles our convictions about who God is, what God wants us to do, and who God wants us to be. We have these two guides at least to direct our understanding and interpretation: the wide diversity of religions in general and our status as a minority within the larger company. The positions we develop should acknowledge our situation and offer clarity for our life together.

To reiterate, my mother asked two simple questions: "When did they put that in there?" and "Why didn't anyone ever tell me?" In the chapters to follow, we will explore a number of biblical passages in light of these questions. Many who have studied the Bible carefully will be led through familiar territory, but the details we will consider have not always been widely or clearly shared. There is ample ground to till that will enable us to grow an understanding of our Christian faith that is quite able to include the diversity that seems to threaten so many. Or perhaps, to use a different metaphor, we may come to see that we are part of a large tapestry of divine design, brilliant and vibrant in all its diverse parts. Our distinct contribution is to be made by coming to an understanding of the richness that is in the Bible and developing the clarity and courage to tell others about what we know. We alone do not constitute the whole tapestry. Along with each of the world's religions, we are a part of God's wondrous weaving, important in our very distinctiveness.

As we listen to the Bible anew, perhaps our eyes and ears may be opened so that we may see more clearly and learn to hear more empathetically with our hearts. At least, that is the goal toward which we set out.

Discussion Questions

1. How have you experienced the decline in the numbers of Christians in North America, locally and nationally? In light of this decline, what are some of the adjustments we need to make in the way we interact with others, both Christians and non-Christians?
2. Elsa Tamez has called for North American Christians to "trade knowledge for emotion." What does she mean? How can we rightly allow "experience" to complement the Bible and theology in our reflection upon God's purposes in our modern world?
3. "We cannot determine what others think about us, but we can and should be clear about how we think about others." How have we misrepresented our Christian heritage? What are some of the changes we might make as we seek a better understanding of ourselves and of others?

PART 2

A New Word

Opening Our Ears

Chapter 4

Hearing with Our Hearts

*T*he Bible, in many places, is shocking! This is one of the things no one told my mother. Certainly, there are words of comfort and encouragement, but there are many more passages that chastise and challenge and confuse and, sometimes, even embarrass. Sometimes the message of the Bible is so demanding that those addressed (ancients and moderns) prefer to act as if they haven't heard, haven't understood. Isaiah 29 preserves one such message.

> Stupefy yourselves and be in a stupor,
>   blind yourselves and be blind!
> Be drunk, but not from wine,
>   stagger, but not from strong drink!
> For the LORD has poured out upon you
>   a spirit of deep sleep;
> He has closed your eyes, you prophets,
>   and covered your heads, you seers.
>   (Isaiah 29:9–10)

> The LORD said:
> Because these people draw near with their mouths
>   and honor me with their lips,
>   while their hearts are far from me,
> and their worship of me is a human commandment learned
>   by rote;
> so I will again do
>   amazing things with this people,
>   shocking and amazing.

The wisdom of their wise shall perish,
and the discernment of the discerning shall be hidden.
(Isaiah 29:13–14)

This is a difficult passage to understand in any positive way. The religious leadership is condemned in no uncertain terms. There is a clear echo of the infamous words of the prophet Isaiah pronouncing unending judgment on his people (see below). These words are found again in the New Testament in condemnation of some of Jesus' contemporaries (Matthew 13:10–17; Mark 4:10–12; Luke 8:9–10). Many Christians across the centuries have interpreted these words as an indictment against not only the Jews of Jesus' day but also Jews living in modern times as well. Is that an appropriate understanding? I think not. But what then? Is there still a "word of the Lord" in these words for us?

We are hardly the first to face the issue of interpretation. Nor are we the first to struggle with the matter of discernment. In 742 BCE the prophet Isaiah was commissioned by God to speak to the people of Judah. In 745 the great Assyrian king Tiglath-pileser III had come to power and initiated an expansion of the Assyrian Empire. As a result, eventually the northern kingdom, Israel, was destroyed, and the southern kingdom, Judah, was severely damaged. The relative calm experienced by both Israel and Judah during the preceding five decades came to an end. The rise of Tiglath-pileser, also called Pul in the Bible (2 Kings 15:19; 2 Chronicles 5:26), radically changed their context. Isaiah's people had to face the direct challenge of Assyrian military power and the claims of a polytheistic religion, a religion that seemed to work, at least if military and economic success were the measures. A new expression of pluralism was at their door.

The prophet Isaiah of Jerusalem was active between 742 and 690 BCE (approximately). He was directed by God to address the royal house of David concerning God's purposes at that time. Isaiah's disciples collected and passed on to us two major groups of oracles and some biographical narratives reflecting Isaiah's work. The first set, found in chapters 2–12 (with some additions from later periods), preserves Isaiah's words to King Ahaz and the people of Judah during the first Assyrian incursion in Palestine, somewhere around 735 BCE. The second set, found in chapters 28–39 (again with some material from later times), contains Isaiah's oracles and counsel to King Hezekiah and the people of Judah during the time leading up to and including the siege of Jerusalem by the Assyrian armies of Sennacherib in 701 BCE.

In Isaiah 6 the commissioning of Isaiah is remembered. Isaiah experienced a vision of God enthroned in the Temple and surrounded by six-winged seraphim. After an exchange between Isaiah and God, which is often considered as the paradigm for a proper confessional liturgy (6:3–7), Isaiah heard and responded to the divine invitation to communicate God's will to the people.

And the message? Not one that any of us covets. Isaiah was told to say to his people:

> Keep listening, but do not comprehend;
> Keep looking, but do not understand.
> (Isaiah 6:9)

Isaiah's charge was to "make the mind of this people dull, and stop their ears, and shut their eyes," thereby assuring their inability to hear and repent (6:10).

Now, I know many a pastor who often feels that they are actively participating in Isaiah's ministry, at least when measured by the degree of understanding and response reflected in the congregation. But I don't know many who want that outcome, and I doubt that Isaiah relished it either. His immediate lament-like response was "How long, O Lord?" (6:11). I think he realized that his was going to be a tough row to hoe. And no doubt a number of you can identify with the prophet on the frustrations of the task!

We know that Isaiah's message in 735 went largely unheeded. King Rezin of Damascus (Syria) and King Pekah of Israel promulgated a rebellion against Assyria. They wanted Ahaz to join their revolt and threatened him if he didn't (7:1–17). Despite the assurances of Isaiah that he need take no action, King Ahaz of Judah, with the support of his advisers and quite possibly of the wider public, called for Assyria's intervention and protection. Isaiah urged Ahaz to be calm, but the king did not listen. His ears were closed. Indeed, as a result of the king's decision, Assyria swept into the land like a mighty flood. The kingdoms of Israel and Aram (Syria) were destroyed, and Judah's autonomy was severely compromised (8:5–10).

So let's return to Isaiah 29 and to a people who neither saw, heard, nor understood. This word was proclaimed some thirty years later than the message to Ahaz and after the commissioning that Isaiah reported in chapter 6. How are we to hear Isaiah's puzzling words? Is no one capable of understanding God's purpose? First, we need to understand that this message was not a word to some vague group living in an unknown time. It was not a word meant for "everyone;" not a message for all people everywhere for all times. No, it was a word to a very specific people in a very specific time. We should not generalize it or universalize it as if it were a philosophical principle of some sort. Nor should we moralize on its basis, thus claiming an ethical guideline or a standard for behavior. But we can ponder the passage; we can reflect on ways we might hear it today.

It began as a word to the people of Judah, God's people, who faced a very difficult situation. When do you trust your leaders and when do you not? How do you determine who to listen to? For how long do you let inertia cripple reform, allow self-interest to stifle justice? Isaiah was certain that the insensitivity and spiritual blindness of the leaders and people of Judah would culminate in disaster. And, in hindsight, the very mission and message he was given (Isaiah 6:9) helped to bring it to pass. The more the people turned a deaf ear to the prophet, the closer they moved toward destruction. But we should remember that Isaiah's word of judgment was not the only message he gave to the people nor was it his last. They could not know at the time—though we do now—that out of their destruction new life was to come. God did indeed do "amazing things," startling wonders.

Thirty years later, in 705 BCE, King Hezekiah of Judah rebelled against Assyria at the beginning of Sennacherib's reign. Perhaps he was emboldened by his perception of Assyrian weakness. Perhaps the official theology of God's eternal commitment to the protection of Jerusalem and David's dynasty prompted him to act (see 2 Samuel 7:8–16; Psalm 89:19–37). No doubt the language of "Immanuel, God with us" was part of the "honor" that was on the lips of the people (Isaiah 7:10–17; 29:13). A century later, in Jeremiah's time, the "commandment learned by rote" took the form of the deceptive assurance: "This is the temple of the LORD, the temple of the LORD, the temple of the LORD" (Jeremiah 7:4; Isaiah 29:13).

Whatever, Hezekiah clearly underestimated how King Sennacherib would react. In 701 BCE the Assyrian army swept through Phoenicia and Philistia. Then, despite support lent Judah by Egypt, the Assyrians wrecked havoc in Judah; forty-six cities were destroyed and a siege was laid around Jerusalem. Exactly what happened next is not clear. Jerusalem was not taken. Perhaps Isaiah's intervention, as well as a plague that devastated the troops, caused the retreat of the Assyrian army (Isaiah 37:33–36; cf. 2 Chronicles 32:20–21). Assyrian records and other verses in Isaiah give reason to think that there may also have been an attempted coup back in Nineveh that required the army's withdrawal (Isaiah 37:37–38). Or perhaps the prayers of Hezekiah were responsible (2 Kings 19:14–34). On the other hand, another source preserved in 2 Kings connects the Assyrian departure to a hefty tribute paid by King Hezekiah to the Assyrians (2 Kings 18:14–16).

However we might understand the exact details, the "escape" of Jerusalem and the healing of Hezekiah became, for many, confirmation of the theological conviction of God's absolute commitment to preserve Jerusalem and the Davidic monarchy, no matter what. As already noted, a century later Jeremiah had to deal with this misinterpretation of divine grace. The inability of the kings and the people of Judah to hear with their ears or to see with their eyes was clear. Their very theology was a stumbling block. What had initially been intended to provide comfort, in fact, apparently made it impossible for them to turn their hearts toward God.

But let's stop and consider this. What did Isaiah's people think was happening in 735 and 705, before the "miracle" of 701? What did they see, hear, or understand? Apparently they understood very little of what Isaiah was concerned about. Injustice, exploitation of the poor, confusion concerning what was culture and what was involved in faithfulness—these matters, so important for the prophet, seem to have been of little significance to the king or the people.

Rather, they saw, heard, and understood the politics of international military power. They saw, heard, and understood the religion of economic success and prosperity. But the wisdom of their wise— and probably their so-called conventional wisdom as well—was considered by most to be unwise. Discernment had become utterly clouded by self-interest, by national myopia, by trusting in human solutions. Religion had been reduced to reciting dogma, making pious assertions of certainty based on the dogma. Their faithlessness was, in fact, demonstrated by the way they dealt with matters that deserved compassion and with people who required assistance. Rather than working for justice with mercy, they acted with hearts as hard as stone. I think we can understand to some measure what was going on in 735 and 705 because at times we are not so terribly different from our religious forebearers.

How can we truly open our eyes and listen with our hearts? How can we jump-start our religious imaginations and move in a new direction? How can we get ready to comprehend *now* the "amazing things" that God is always capable of doing? The people of Judah sat in the darkness of their closed minds, their atrophied religious imaginations. Will we sit with them? Or will we respond to the challenge of Thomas Friedman cited in the opening chapter and use our religious imaginations in a positive way to sketch out a new path? Are we doomed to an uncaring, unfaithful response?

As I consider my own context, several insights emerge. First, I am in no position to declare a word of judgment to the people of the United States as a whole, though at times I certainly would like to do so. Sometimes the things that some people do seem so utterly stupid to me that I want to level a blast against them designed to set them straight, but that is not mine to do. Sometimes I feel so morally and intellectually superior that I forget my limitations and my own biases. Then I remember a warning penned by columnist Leonard Pitts of the *Miami Herald*. Responding to a series of hate messages he had received as a result of one of his columns, he chastised all who "mouth pious hatreds with a smug certitude and offhand arrogance accessible only to the deeply, profoundly and utterly wrong" (2007, H5). I am not a prophet, and I need to remember that.

No, I need to start with a much more particular audience: namely my own rather small part of the church of Jesus Christ. What has my denomination not seen or heard or understood? Unfortunately, the list is long. For the most part, we have not actually seen the desperation of the undocumented poor that impels them to risk life and limb to come to the United States for the sake of a five-dollar-an-hour job. Nor have we clearly heard the cries of futility and the growing anxiety among those within our so-called working poor who for several years have experienced a loss of real income and faced the growing threat of serious illness without sufficient medical insurance.

At another level, we have not chosen to acknowledge the rapidly developing diversity of the larger population within which we live, which makes some of our cherished theological convictions seem rather quaint if not totally irrelevant. A philosophical explication of the doctrine of double predestination is not a pressing issue for most church members, to say anything of the multitudes beyond! The list of irrelevant—at least to the context in which we live—theological trivia can easily be extended. Our church rulebooks are not going to redeem anyone! So, we need first of all to recognize that *we* may well be those who do not see or hear or understand. More pointedly, we who are leaders have too often preferred the certainties and securities of the status quo rather than looking for the "amazing things" that God intends. We need to face up to our unwillingness to attend to what God desires.

That brings us to a second point upon which we should reflect. Isaiah's message was not without some measure of hope. God did, and continues to do, amazing and unexpected things. We need to work at opening our eyes, and those of our people, so that we may see those things. The growing religious diversity in our communities, in our world, that is so real does not have to be seen as a threat. Reaching out to work with different people, joining those of other faiths in conversation, rethinking our theology in light of our changing circumstances, seeing and understanding the new context that God is creating all around us—all these actions can be invigorating and renewing. Yes, things will change, but that does not mean things will necessarily be worse. "Telling it like it is" is imperative, but that should not be an act of negative judgment so much as an act of critical evaluation. Telling it like it is, seeing it like it truly is, can and should lead to changes of correction and enhancement.

Third, if this text in Isaiah 29 does actually address me/us, then I/we are challenged to seek discernment. Since the people refused to listen, understanding was "hidden" in Isaiah's time, but ours is a different time, a different context. Certainly we should be warned by ancient Judah's situation, but we are not necessarily destined to a similar predicament. We do have a choice, a choice to try to open our eyes and ears, the possibility of developing listening and compassionate hearts, and that is what can make discernment possible. We need to reexamine our traditions to determine where the real "eye-openers" and "mind-blowers" are to be found.

We will need to do some tearing down in the course of building up. We live in a context of mushrooming diversity, which is immensely threatening for some. We can "circle the wagons," as Isaiah's people apparently did, or we can trust anew in God's promises to do new and amazing things. The words of the Bible address us, not just the people of Isaiah's time or those of Jesus' day. But they must be interpreted in the present context. Interpretations passed down from preceding generations may be instructive, but they may also be wrong, at least in our new context of diversity. We have to have enough courage and trust in God to try to find new "answers" for our contemporary questions. And we have to talk about all of this with our mothers!

Discussion Questions

1. How can very particular words (like those of Isaiah) be heard appropriately by people living decades or even centuries later? What might it mean to listen anew with our hearts?

2. As we struggle with the message of Isaiah, in what ways does that ancient word both chastise and challenge us? Have we been guilty of closing our eyes to the realities of growing religious pluralism? What can we do about this?

3. What are some of the "issues" that may distract us from our real work as Christians in North America? What are some of the questions being asked by the young, the unchurched, and the doubters in your community that deserve honest discussion? How can we get in step with facing current issues without forsaking our traditions?

Chapter 5

Embarrassing Particularity

*I*n every religious tradition are some texts that are offensive or at least embarrassing. Generally, it is the particularity of an ancient text that is so troublesome. Such passages present real people in difficult situations, voicing strident or anguished sentiments that are often painful for us to hear. We find such statements difficult to consider as revelatory. In this chapter and the next, I intend to explore a few biblical passages that for most modern Christian readers fall into this category, passages that some have termed "harsh texts." The aim is to see how contextual interpretation may lead to a reconsideration of the intention of these passages, and thereby perhaps a new understanding of them. I do so with the deep conviction that Jesus Christ is in himself the most generous and the most particular of all "texts" and desires that we find his truth, an inclusive and not exclusive truth, as we ponder the riches of our tradition.

Let's begin by going back to Isaiah as remembered in Mark. In response to a question from his disciples concerning his use of parables, according to Mark, Jesus said:

> To you has been given the secret of the kingdom of God, but for those outside, everything comes in parables; in order that
>
> "they may indeed look, but not perceive,
>   and may indeed listen, but not understand;
> so that they may not turn again and be forgiven."
>   (Mark 4:11–12; compare
>   Isaiah 6:9–10; 29:13–14)

39

The other two Synoptic Gospels, Matthew and Luke, make similar though perhaps less harsh use of these words from Isaiah (Matthew 13:10–17; Luke 8:9–10). The primary aim seems to have been to assure Jesus' small band of followers that they were right to believe in him. Other Jews might not respond—after all, so it had been in Isaiah's day—but Jesus' disciples were on target with their positive commitment to him.

In Acts, Luke goes a bit further in interpreting Jesus' use of Isaiah's words by quoting them to support a dramatic declaration: "Let it be known to you then that this salvation of God has been sent to the Gentiles; they will listen" (Acts 28:28; cf. the Syrophoenician woman in Mark 7:24–30; Matthew 15:21–28). And John concludes his review of Jesus' public ministry by using Isaiah's words to explain why the majority of the people had not responded to all the many signs Jesus had done in their midst. John then added, however, that "many, even of the [Judean] authorities, believed in him. But because of the Pharisees they did not confess it, for fear that they would be put out of the synagogue; for they loved human glory more than the glory that comes from God" (John 12:42–43).

While both Acts and John reflect the growing tension within the Jewish community of the first century, between the Jews who did follow Jesus and those who did not, neither explicitly says that all Jews are rejected by God. Earlier Paul had vigorously denied such a conclusion (see Romans 9–11). But in subsequent Christian interpretation, such a conclusion was reached and defended—repeatedly—for nearly two thousand years. The rejection of the Jews as a people became an unquestioned premise for millions of Christians. The language of "Christ killers" and "deicide race" and the "teaching of contempt" became an accepted norm for all too many by which to castigate Jews. Implicit in this condemnation of Jews, of course, is the rejection of *all* others who do not follow Jesus.

In light of my/our current context, diversity and pluralism are pressing issues. How shall I interpret this tradition associated with Isaiah and Jesus? I think that it is critical for us to remember the historical context in which these texts were first written. Jewish Jews, Christian Jews, Gentile Christians, perhaps some "Gentile Jews"/"God fearers"—all were actively engaged in seeking to live out God's way, but all constituted *very small minorities* within the vast Roman Empire.

They were much more concerned about their *own* relationship with God rather than the relationship others might enjoy. The question was, Does God love *us*? The question was not, Has God rejected *them*?

In the Gospels, even in John, the issue is clear that some Judeans, particularly some of the leaders, had rejected Jesus. Their eyes, ears, and hearts were not open to his call. John is the most explicit on this point, but John does not suggest that God has rejected all Jews. Remember, all of Jesus' initial followers were Jews. Even when Luke announced that God's salvation was being sent to the Gentiles, to those not originally understood as part of God's people—though the stories of Noah (see Genesis 9) and Abraham (see Genesis 12) clearly teach otherwise—Luke did not declare that God's love was thereby removed from the Jews. God's salvation is large enough to extend to the whole human family, to Jews and to Gentiles.

Reflecting upon human history, it seems that people need to have "enemies." The early Christians, unfortunately, were no exception. First these passages were used against some particular Jewish leaders and some particular synagogues. Some Christian leaders, from as early as the second century, produced some virulent anti-Jewish pronouncements and sermons, based in part on Isaiah's words as they understood them to have been used by Jesus. Herein began the development of the previously mentioned theological doctrine known as "supersessionism," holding that the church had displaced and superseded the people of Israel as the people of God. After Emperor Constantine in effect "established" Christianity in 324 CE as the principal religion of the Roman Empire, the doctrine of Christian supersessionism really began to take hold. And with it, the whole apparatus of government was used to support its required orthodoxy.

But the use of these words to defame and attack others was not confined to Christian diatribes against Jews. In the sixteenth century, a new twist of interpretation took place. Calvin and others turned Isaiah 29:13 against the Roman Church. It was the pope and the Roman hierarchy who only honored God "with their lips, while their hearts are far from me," and whose "worship of me is a human commandment learned by rote." It should be noted, by the way, that Calvin was doing a form of contextual interpretation. He was sensitive to his context and sought God's word for his time and place. I seriously question his conclusions, but I honor his effort. He still has much to teach us.

But let's go a different direction. Other texts give insight into a different kind of anti-Jewish and anti-Muslim prejudice widespread among Christians. This "exclusivistic" view parades behind the idea of the progressive-evolution-of-religion promoted by the Enlightenment. Psalm 137 provides a good example. Produced in response to being taken captive as exiles to Babylon in 587/586 BCE, it is a touching song of lament for a lost land, a song reflective of the Judean experience of oppressive exile.

> By the rivers of Babylon—
>   there we sat down and there we wept
>   when we remembered Zion.
> On the willows there
>   we hung our harps.
> For there our captors
>   asked us for songs,
> and our tormentors asked for mirth, saying,
>   "Sing us one of the songs of Zion."
>   (Psalm 137:1–3)

Hearing these words evokes sympathy, perhaps even empathy. To be torn from one's homeland is an awful experience, which no one desires. Lamentation is appropriate and understandable.

The conclusion is equally dramatic but has a different effect on many:

> O daughter Babylon, you devastator!
>   Happy shall they be who pay you back
>   what you have done to us!
> Happy shall they be who take your little ones
>   and dash them against the rock!
>   (Psalm 137:8–9)

Such harsh words offend the ears and the hearts of many Christians! Where is the recognition that the sins of the elders should not be visited upon the children? Where is the forgiveness of one's enemies? Where are common human decency and a regard for human rights? Or at an even more immediate level, where is good taste?

Psalm 137 is not alone in the First Testament in expressing "negative" attitudes. In Joshua 6:21 we read: "Then they [Joshua's troops] devoted to destruction by the edge of the sword all in the city [Jericho], both men and women, young and old, oxen, sheep, and donkeys." Such texts as these have been marshaled forth as demonstration of the "inferior" character of the whole Old Testament and the "primitive" character of the "god" of the Old Testament as well. A Christian leader, Marcion, who lived in the second century CE, used such arguments to advocate the rejection of the First Testament as unworthy of inclusion in the Christian Bible. He is remembered as one of the first to champion such a view, but he was hardly the last.

The argument is rather specious, in my opinion, but I have heard it for years and years and from many people who, it seems to me, should know better. For many Christians the Old Testament is considered a burden. They view the "god" of the Old Testament as an inferior deity, vindictive and harsh, the creation of the adherents of a primitive religion. The evidence? The violence voiced in passages like Psalm 137 and Joshua 6.

The argument goes that any people, in this instance the Israelites, who would suggest that God could in any way condone or, even worse, command such actions, simply must be wrong. And if they are wrong about one thing, they could be wrong about everything. Thus the Old Testament and the God of the Old Testament should be rejected as primitive, inferior, and useless to those who have seen the true light: Christians. Christianity, on the other hand, though certainly not perfect, is more advanced, more humane, simply more "modern." Religion is evolving, we are told, and the Old Testament and the understanding of God expressed there are simply outdated, obsolete. And of course, if you reject the reality of the God of the First Testament, the people who claimed to be chosen by that God can also easily be dismissed and perhaps even exterminated if worse comes to worst.

Mahmoud Ahmadinejad, the president of Iran, has denied the historicity of the Holocaust, the slaughter of millions of European Jews as well as nearly 5 million other European civilians. At the same time he has called for another slaughter, this time of millions of Middle Eastern Jews, by urging the destruction of modern Israel, all in the name of justice and religion. He has denied that he really wants to kill them all; rather, he only wants to remove them forcibly to some other place, somewhere in the West. Whatever he finally means, his rhetoric is inflammatory, to say the least. His history is wacky. His motives are transparently self-serving. But his intentions are serious and should not be taken lightly. What's more—and this is the real tragedy—he voices the feelings of many, many Middle Easterners, Muslims and Christians, who openly or secretly would applaud the annihilation of the nation Israel. And there are many in the West, unfortunately, who also would take some large measure of satisfaction in such a disaster.

We should also pause to reflect on the theological assumption implicit in this line of reasoning: that which is "old" or not in keeping with "modern Western sensibilities" is declared wrong and not worthy of consideration. Such an attitude can invalidate all but the most recent religious traditions. Not only the religion of the ancient Israelites but also religions of the early Christians, Muslims, Buddhists, Hindus, and others are disqualified because they are "primitive" and do not reflect a "modern" understanding of the world. Such an approach, it seems to me, is far too sweeping in its scope and shows a large degree of ignorance and arrogance with respect to the particular religions that are in question.

Let's return to the particulars of Psalm 137. If we lived as a very small minority of people exiled by a military power like Babylon, known for its cruelty, we too might feel somewhat hostile. Or if we lived within a culture that held hate-filled attitudes toward us, we too might sometimes feel just a little such animosity toward our enemies. The Jews in modern Israel number about 7 million. The Muslims in the surrounding countries number around 350 million. Think about it. And the relative number of Jewish exiles who sang and remembered Psalm 137 was equally small in comparison to the Babylonian population into which they were thrust. What is remarkable about Psalm 137 is not that there is an expression of hostility toward the enemy. What is noteworthy is the candid honesty before God by which the exiles voiced their hatred!

Of course, no one can applaud as virtuous the notion of slaughtering little children, and that brings us to our own context. What do we do with Psalm 137? First, I hope we have learned that simply because something negative is expressed in Scripture doesn't mean that God endorses it, especially if it is in a human prayer such as a psalm. Further, if the God of the First Testament is indeed the "God and Father of our Lord Jesus Christ," then difficult texts, like this psalm and Joshua 6, must be read in that light. Whatever the passages may say, they must be heard within the gracious love revealed in our Lord Jesus and in many passages in the Old Testament as well, passages such as Exodus 34 and Hosea 11.

Second, while honesty requires an admission that sometimes, just sometimes, we wouldn't mind seeing some of our enemies get it in the neck, we are also reminded that such judgment is not ours to administer! The Judean exiles, forcibly domiciled in Babylon, had neither the power nor the opportunity to retaliate against their enemies. They were not considering such actions nor even thinking such thoughts. A hostile response was not even a temptation! But Psalm 137 provided them strong words to express their negative feelings before God, and that is important. They had the feelings—God knew they had the feelings—and they needed to express them. Only as they voiced their deep anguish and anger could they move on, confidently leaving the desired judgment in the hands of the Divine.

We also need such words on occasion, or at least I do. I may not want the utter destruction of my enemies, but a badly sprained ankle or a significant drop in some of their stocks would be okay. I need to own my own negative feelings and express them before God.

More seriously, what do we learn from Psalm 137 about our context? There was a time when a Christian "majority" could (and did) dictate civil policy in many parts of North America. It did not even require an actual plurality of voters, only a concentration of power. I recently read that somewhere around 47 percent of American voters want to see the government impose "Christian values" on the nation. That is scary! Partly because such folks are totally out of touch with constitutional realities and partly because they think there is agreement about what those "Christian values" might look like. We couldn't dictate such policies even if we wanted to!

Diana Eck, Harvard theologian and professor of comparative religion, has amassed an enormous amount of data that has led her to say that the United States is the most religiously pluralistic nation in the world (Eck 2001). The number and variety of Buddhist "denominations" to be found in southern California, for instance, is greater than in any other part of the world. Other studies of the most recent census indicate that there are almost 2 million more Mormons now living in the United States than there are members of the Presbyterian Church (U.S.A.). There are almost three times as many atheists/agnostics in the United States than the number of Presbyterians, and they are second only to the Roman Catholics in percentage of growth since the previous survey. The point of such statistics is that even if "we" (whoever that might be) wanted to and could—and there are still a number of communities where it is clearly possible—impose "our" values on others, it would be very unwise, at least if we want to live together peaceably in the future.

What has this to do with Psalm 137? Well, perhaps the concern we should have is not with whether this psalm expresses some "unchristian" feelings. Rather, the questions rightly are these: What are the feelings that we have evoked in others by the misuse of our political advantage here and during the years of colonialism, which we endorsed around the world? Who would like to see our children bashed against the wall, and is there any justification for such feelings? Why are others so suspicious of "Christian America" when we try to share our views about their cultures? Do Muslims have any reason to fear us just because our forebears inflicted two hundred years of calamity on them with repeated Crusades against them centuries ago and with military assistance (and sometimes preemptive attack) that has helped keep the Middle East in turmoil for the past half century?

The point is that there are clearly passages in the Bible (and in the Qur'an as well) that have led Jews, Christians, and Muslims to relate to others in a negative rather than positive manner. In the historical traditions of each group are events demonstrating the harshness that can result from an uncritical, unreasoned reading of its holy writings, particularly when any particular group has a majority position over others. When we remember that the foundational texts (all of them in each tradition) were written by people who lived in and had the perspective of being in a minority, we can then hear the texts more clearly. The Gospels, Acts, and Psalm 137 express some strong feelings that were experienced in very particular circumstances. We, too, though it is embarrassing to admit, may have some of these same feelings on occasion in our multicultural, multinational, religiously diversified world. We need to admit them, yes, but we should not harbor them, nourish them, nor act on them. Psalm 137 didn't instruct the ancient Judean exiles to carry out their feelings of hatred against their tormentors, and it doesn't tell us to do so either! Minorities can't afford such action, and majorities shouldn't! Moreover, my mom would have had nothing to do with such behavior if she knew it was going on and if she had had the Bible appropriately interpreted to her!

Discussion Questions

1. What difference does it make in understanding the use of Isaiah's words in the Gospels and Acts when the minority social status of the early church is taken into consideration? How did interpretation move from a very particular point to an abstract, universal application? How do you hear these texts?
2. How has the notion of a progressive evolution of religion led to very exclusive and prejudiced opinions about non-Christian religions? What is problematic about the widespread notion that the God of the Old Testament is a God of wrath and the God of the New Testament a God of grace?
3. Recognizing that there is indeed harshness expressed in Psalm 137, what are some of the "positive" themes that the psalm does nonetheless suggest? Have you ever felt some of the negative feelings the psalmist shares? What are some of the ways we may have caused others to wish us ill?

Chapter 6

In Jesus' Name

*I*n his award-winning book *The Dignity of Difference,* Rabbi Jonathan Sacks, the chief rabbi of the United Hebrew Congregations of Britain and the Commonwealth, wrote:

> Every great faith has within it harsh texts which, read literally, can be taken to endorse narrow particularism, suspicion of strangers, and intolerance toward those who believe differently than we do. Every great faith also has within it sources that emphasize kinship with the stranger, empathy with the outsider, the courage that leads people to extend a hand across boundaries of estrangement or hostility. The choice is ours. Will the generous texts of our traditions serve as interpretative keys to the rest, or will the abrasive passages determine our ideas of what we are and what we are called to do? (2002, 207–8)

In my opinion a text is "abrasive" if it fosters animosity toward others, whether they are believers or nonbelievers. Rabbi Sacks encourages us to turn to the more-positive texts in our tradition, and we will do so. But before we do, we will consider one other set of passages that many consider "harsh" and exclusive in tone. Many Christians I know prefer to ignore this account with the hope that it will go away: Acts 5:1–11, the story of Ananias and Sapphira. But there are others who latch on to it as a model for the way the church should be governed, and that makes it problematic. In either instance, the text remains for us to consider.

This story is "harsh" in a different way than the texts considered in the preceding chapter. When taken out of context and interpreted literally, this passage has been used to promote a culture in the church that is legalistic and to support an attitude toward "outsiders" that discounts them as worthless in the eyes of God. Such a stance is certainly detrimental to living peaceably with others in a religiously pluralistic world.

The story, found in Acts 5 in the New Testament, is part of a longer section that begins at 3:1 and extends to 5:42. The "last act," so to speak, is the story of a man and woman who were members of a congregation led by Peter. The story is simple enough. Ananias and his wife, Sapphira, sold a piece of property and decided to give the proceeds to the church. But then, according to the text, because Satan led them to lie "to the Holy Spirit" (Acts 5:3), Ananias brought only a portion of the proceeds as a gift to the church. Peter, however, by the power of the Holy Spirit, recognized that Ananias was not telling the truth.

At first Peter gave Ananias the opportunity to set things right and tell the truth about the return from his sale. But again Ananias lied about the amount of the sale and thus about the worth of the gift. No sooner were the words out of his mouth than he fell down dead, presumably by the power of the Holy Spirit, though the text does not actually say so. Ananias was immediately taken out and buried. Three hours later his wife came in, not knowing that Ananias had died for their deception. Sapphira was questioned about the matter, and she continued the lie! Thus, she too immediately fell dead. The passage concludes: "And great fear seized the whole church and all who heard of these things" (5:11).

I can imagine that there are times, particularly when there is a budget crunch, when some leaders might wish to have such power over the members of their congregations. How many pledges are made and never completed! How sanctimonious can some "big givers" behave! Oh that they might simply drop dead—if they have included the church in their wills. Echoes of Psalm 137?

Most of us, though, don't like the passage for the same reasons we don't like the story of Achan's transgression in Joshua 7, with the subsequent punishment that was visited upon him and his household. For one thing, I suspect that we don't really think it is fair. Evoke a confession, take the amount that has been withheld, and get on with it! After all, Ananias didn't have to give the church anything! People shouldn't have to die for a little cheating. Don't we all cheat just a little now and then? And besides, does God operate that way? We certainly hope not. A passage like this suggests a view of God that few of us share. It becomes an embarrassment, a passage we hope other folks do not find or ask about.

Further, it can promote a kind of legalism that can stifle a congregation. If we start looking over the shoulders of one another, trying to guess who the next Ananias or Sapphira might be, we will be in trouble for sure. A sense of fear might well seize us all and, at least for many Christians I know, the only safe action in such a circumstance is no action at all. But we certainly don't want that; goodness knows that we have enough inaction already! This text is disturbing, "harsh," because the "justice" that it seems to promote is so rigid, so unbending, so mechanical. Where is the mercy of God upon which all of us are so dependent?

If we are to understand this text in a way that may help us rather than shackle us, we need to consider the context of this story. We do well not to take it out of its original setting and try to "apply" it directly to our contemporary situation. First of all, the story was intended to promote loyalty and dedication among a small group of Christians in difficult, threatening circumstances. Christians, and Jews for that matter, as previously noted, constituted a very small percentage of the population of the Roman Empire in the first and second centuries CE. The underlying message for the Christians to whom Acts was addressed was, "If you want to sign up with this group, you had better be serious." That is not a bad message even for us today, but for the early church it was a necessity. Lack of loyalty and dedication, in the face of the opposition of the empire, could indeed be deadly.

Remember that the story of Ananias and Sapphira is situated in the midst of a section of Acts several chapters in length, beginning at 3:1 and continuing through 5:42. To understand it, we need to review the wider context. These chapters describe the early ministry of healing and teaching carried on by Peter and some of the other apostles. In this part of Acts, all the activity is among Jews and directed to Jews. It takes place at Solomon's Portico at the Temple (3:11). One particular crippled beggar was carried in (3:2). After a brief exchange with the lame man, Peter declared him healed (3:6). This act of mercy provided the occasion, then, for Peter to explain the power by which he was able to heal the man: the power of "the name of Jesus" (3:6).

Now the problem for the authorities, apparently, was not the theological witness to Jesus that Peter made. Certainly the Sadducees were "much annoyed" at the suggestion that "in Jesus there is resurrection of the dead" (4:2). But the real concern centered on the fact that Peter had "healed" a lame beggar. The authorities were quite perplexed. Included in the opposition were some of "the priests, the captain of the temple, and the Sadduccees" (4:1), and subsequently, as well, the "rulers, elders, Annas the high priest, Caiaphas, John, and Alexander, and all who were of the high-priestly family" (4:5–6). Indeed, a "family" affair! They wanted to know by "what power or by what name did you [Peter] do this?" (4:7). The authorities were exercised over the question of "power," who had the right to do things such as healing in their community.

Peter responded by saying: "Rulers of the people and elders, if we are questioned today because of a good deed done to someone who was sick and are asked how this man has been healed, let it be known to all of you, and to all the people of Israel, that this man is standing before you in good health by the name of Jesus Christ of Nazareth, whom you crucified, whom God raised from the dead" (4:8b–10). After this testimony by Peter, the summary statement of the unit follows: "There is salvation in no one else, for there is no other name under heaven given among mortals by which we must be saved" (4:12).

Two things, at least, are very important to note about this summary declaration. First, the words translated "salvation" (Greek *sōtēria*) and "saved" in 4:12 are variants from the same word that in 4:9 is translated "healed." To "heal" people was to rescue them, to "save" them from ill health, to preserve them from grave difficulty. The terms "salvation" and "healing" in this passage mean practically the same thing. It is only when 4:12 is lifted out of context that *sōtēria* begins to be considered as a theological category. Then the text may become divisive, suggesting that only Christians can experience "salvation." That is not what the sentence means in its literary context. In Acts, the simplest understanding of the verse is that Peter healed a man by the power of Jesus' name, the only name that Peter would claim. Peter was not saying that he alone could assist in healing, but he was insisting that when he, Peter, did so, it was by the power of Jesus' name, not by some magical power that Peter himself possessed.

Cynthia Campbell, seminary president and theologian, draws upon the work of New Testament scholar Beverly Gaventa and makes this comment on Acts 4:12:

> Beverly Gaventa points out that the phrase "by which we must be saved" is an attempt to render the Greek *dei,* "it is necessary." Luke in particular uses this word for things that happen in accordance with God's will. The force of Peter's claim is that it is through God's will that the name of Jesus brings healing or salvation. Thus, Gaventa concludes, "In context, the emphasis falls on God's gift of salvation rather than on a negation of other religious practices." This text *does* make a powerful claim about the healing/saving power of the name of Jesus. It does not necessarily mean that God could not or would not work in the lives of human beings by other means. (2007, 48–49)

This latter point brings us to the second important matter. In Peter's day there were many healers and many so-called "mysteries" that competed for the attention of people. One act of healing was not all that noteworthy. Only among the Jewish authorities who were concerned lest God might be blasphemed or that Roman authority might be challenged was there any great consternation. The "notable sign" could not be denied (4:16), so the Jewish leaders dismissed Peter and John with a warning not to speak anymore in Jesus' name, a warning that Peter and John, of course, refused to heed (4:17–20).

The point of this long digression concerning the literary and social context of the story about Ananias and Sapphira, is to demonstrate that the issue for the early church was one of loyalty to the movement. From Peter's declaration of his healing "power" to the deception and death of Ananias and Sapphira, that was the concern. The Christians were a small and vulnerable community that needed encouragement and assurance. Jesus was the source of their "healing," their "preservation," their "salvation." Others questioned what had happened to them, and some of them were cast out of their families and synagogues, but their struggles were all internal to their own community. They did not have an issue about what others believed. They were concerned about their own faith.

A similar "problem" is resolved when John 14:6 is kept in context. That verse reads: "Jesus said to him [Thomas], 'I am the way, and the truth, and the life. No one comes to the Father except through me.'" This verse has been used over the years to exclude others. Some have argued that this verse means that only Christians (and usually only Christians of a certain sort) can experience God's redemptive love. When one examines the context in which this verse is located, however, it seems rather clear that this was not intended as a declaration of universal truth. Rather, it is a very specific response to a very particular group of people: Jesus' disciples.

As with the writer of Acts, for the writer of John the issue was not primarily one of doctrinal correctness. The context makes clear that the issue was a matter of encouraging and maintaining loyalty within the company of disciples who had chosen to follow Jesus. As I have written elsewhere,

> These words are not policy statements. They reflect the rhetoric of conflict, and the struggle of a movement—very much a minority movement at the time—to account for itself and to survive. They provide encouragement and challenge for Christians to be faithful to the God whose way is exemplified in the ministry of Jesus. These words do not define how Christians should understand others but how Christians should structure their own commitments and priorities. (2005, 104)

The early Christians, to reiterate, were not concerned to invalidate the convictions of others. Their main concern was to validate and testify to their own experience. From Peter's "healing"—remember that the term used is one we often translate as "salvation"—of the beggar in Acts 4 to the conclusion of the section in Acts 5, the issue is, "How shall the community share its experience of God?" In John the issue is, "Can we who have followed Jesus be certain of God's love?"

What can we learn from this testimony? First, who are we, and how strong is our own commitment to the church of Jesus Christ? We are people who have been to some measure "healed" but are we concerned to share the "healing" with others? To share my story of healing, however, does not require that I deny the healing that someone else has experienced. We can all marvel when any of us is restored to good health. Second, the change in our circumstance from that of the early church is critical. We now have a long history of dealing with people of other faiths from a position of power. Unfortunately, that history has not always been very noble. Passages like those we have considered here, and particularly the words from Acts 4 and those in the Gospel of John, have been often used in terribly destructive ways to discount others and deny their experience of the divine.

Chris Elwood, theology professor at Louisville Presbyterian Seminary, offered some important reflections on Acts 4:12 in a sermon he preached there in Winn Chapel several years ago (May 2000). Here are a few of his comments:

> Obviously, a simple declaration can have very different meanings (and consequences) when you change the context. That is true for Peter's statement as well. "No Other Name" can be a genuine response to the encounter with Christ or it can be something else. It can be a vital expression of the liberating experience of faith, or it can be a means of setting up a game with special rules that only we can play, a language game that denies the authenticity of experiences that don't conform to the rules of our experience. "No Other Name," when spoken from power to powerlessness, seems to corrupt the good news. "No Other Name," when spoken from the center to the margins, is no longer an echo of Peter's meaning in Acts. "No Other Name," when spoken to boost *our* flagging spirits when we are wearied by the multitude of witnesses to faith, or when it is used to beat down others so that they can see how much better things are over here, corrupts rather than expresses faith.

And again:

> I don't think faith in Christ needs to be an expression of anxiety, born out of the sense of the rarity of redemption—a scarcity of spiritual goods. The experiences that God is in Jesus need not close us off from learning more about the dimensions of God's self-disclosure to the world. Above all, faith in Christ expresses itself in generous love, a love that opens us up to the world and to our friends, as different as they may be. I don't believe Christian love demands that we translate the particular way God has spoken to us into a denial of the religious experience of those who are not Christian. (unpublished)

I agree! Rather than beating others over the head with "harsh texts," let's look for allies, for any and all, who demonstrate the love of God in their lives. In the words of Jesus remembered by both Mark (9:40) and Luke (9:50): "Whoever is not against us is for us." (Yes, I know that Matthew 12:30 has a negative version, but let's stick with the positive.) We need to find and cultivate those who will love others as God has loved them. To help us, we may utilize a number of biblical passages that testify to the generously wide love of God. In the next chapters we will explore some of these "generous" texts with the aim of opening our eyes and hearts to the ongoing work of God in bringing wholeness (salvation) to the world. My mother would be glad, though probably somewhat surprised!

Discussion Questions

1. What insights does the context provide about the story of Ananias and Sapphira? What are some of the differences in understanding of Acts 4:12 that emerge when the verse is read in its literary context?
2. How can reading a passage contextually affect the way a text like John 14:6 is heard? Why is it important to reflect on what a text does not say when trying to talk about what it does say?
3. It is unsettling for many to hear that interpretations of certain biblical passages, long unquestionably accepted, might need reinterpretation. How can the reality of such feelings be recognized and fairly considered? How does the Bible, despite changing interpretations across the ages, nonetheless truly witness to the faithfulness of God?

Chapter 7

Borrowing over the Cultural Fence

David Quammen, noted author on natural history and island bio-geography (among other things), has in his writings brought together an engaging literary style with a great deal of firsthand data on the state of numerous species around the globe. In his book *Monster of God,* Quammen surveys the status of a number of the large "man-eating" animals he calls "alpha predators" (lions, bears, crocodiles, tigers) and worries about their (apparently) rapidly approaching extinction. But in the course of this book, Quammen also relates the actual physical reality about which he writes with the psychic reality or the mythic reality that great fearsome beasts have in the lives of human beings. It is a fascinating study.

In the opening chapter Quammen notes the prominent role of "memorable monsters from ancient Babylonian poetry (Humbaba in the Epic of Gilgamesh, Tiamat in *Enuma Elish*)" as well as elsewhere, in much later medieval literature, for instance (Grendel in *Beowulf,* the wormy dragons in Iceland's *The Saga of the Volsungs*). He then remarks:

> Scripture is another matter. Scriptural monsters tend to have didactic purposes, not just lurid narrative roles. And certain instances combine the didactic with the lurid especially well. Stepping past the lions mentioned in Job 4 and elsewhere—which, though fearsome enough, are ordinary animals of no outsize scale or unearthly menace—I come to the real bugaboo of all the monsters portrayed in the Bible, the archetype of alpha predators: Leviathan." (2003, 10)

Quammen correctly understands the role of Leviathan, especially as described in Job 41. There are references or allusions to this part-dragon, part-crocodile beast in several places in the Bible (Job 3:8; Psalms 74:13–14; 104:26; Isaiah 27:1; see also Job 26:12–13, where the creature is given the name Rahab, as in Psalm 89:10 and Isaiah 51:9), but the only extended description is in Job 41. There is "terror all around its [Leviathan's] teeth. Its back is made of shields in rows, shut up closely as with a seal" (41:14–15). Fire and smoke shoot out of Leviathan's nostrils and mouth (41:19–20). "When it raises itself up the gods are afraid; at the crashing they are beside themselves" (41:25). In conclusion, the Joban text comments simply, "On earth it has no equal, a creature without fear. It surveys everything that is lofty; it is king over all that are proud" (41:33–34). And the purpose of this alpha predator superb? As Quammen puts it:

> The point is that Leviathan, though awesome and dreadful, owes its existence to the Lord himself. *I made this monstrous beast. No one is brave enough or reckless enough to tangle with it. Who then can stand before me?* The role of Leviathan, here in Job 41 and elsewhere in the Bible, was to keep people humble. (13)

David Quammen then goes on to observe:

> Meanwhile, real animals with big teeth and long claws were accomplishing the same thing. For as long as *Homo sapiens* has been sapient—for much longer if you count the evolutionary wisdom stored in our genes—alpha predators have kept us acutely aware of our membership within the natural world. They've done it by reminding us that to them we're just another flavor of meat. (13)

The rest of Quammen's extraordinary study is not of immediate interest here, though his exploration of the Gilgamesh story and that of Beowulf is quite thought provoking (255–69). What intrigues me about his observations in relation to what we are considering here, however, is the amount of "borrowing" that has gone on across the centuries between various ethnic and national groups. There are several places in the Bible where such interaction between the biblical writers and their wider culture seems clearly to have taken place with no great ado. These are worth exploring because they suggest the ways that minorities did and may connect with the thought and literature of others, even with the majorities within which they exist.

Some four to five hundred years before Israel was established in the land of Canaan (somewhere around 1450 BCE), Leviathan appeared in Canaanite literature, in a poem that celebrated the exploits of the storm god Baal. A text has been found at a site located on the coast of what is now Syria, Ras Shamra, known in antiquity as Ugarit, which is approximately 3,500 years old. There are many points at which the Ugaritic literature has proved helpful in better understanding the Bible, especially in terms of language and poetic style. Equally important is the fact that in this literature we see the struggles of the god Baal and the goddess Anat, for instance, placed into a poetic, literary context that offers insight into how they were viewed and honored. That is important because there are numerous references to Baal and other Canaanite deities in the Old Testament.

In one Ugaritic text is a passage that reports Baal's victory over Yam, the god of the sea. Yam is pictured as a seven-headed, slippery, twisting sea serpent. The terminology used is near to that found in Isaiah 27:1, where "evil" is portrayed as the dragon "Leviathan the fleeing serpent, Leviathan the twisting serpent," the dragon God will slay in the sea (see also Isaiah 51:9–10; Psalm 74:13). The linguistic parallels are too close to be accidental. In the Ugaritic text, Baal overcomes the hostile and elusive sea serpent, the embodiment of Yam (cf. Driver 1956, 102–3), part of an annual cycle of victories ascribed to Baal and celebrated. In Isaiah, the Lord God of Israel will at the end of time destroy the serpent Leviathan, which represents all the evil forces resisting the will of God in the present world.

It is somewhat startling to find a text in a non-Israelite mythological poem basically being quoted in a later Israelite prophetic text. What it suggests to me is that it was okay to employ images developed by others to express one's own concerns. Centuries later, in the eighteenth century of the Common Era, Charles Wesley (brother of John Wesley, the founder of Methodism) produced some of the best-loved hymns in the English-speaking world (and actually beyond, in places colonized and evangelized by Europeans and North Americans). One of his primary approaches was to take tunes popular among the general population—drinking songs, in some instances—and provide new words to express a different message. In a similar manner, biblical writers "borrowed" images and terminology, used in one religious setting by their neighbors, for their own purposes in a different setting.

The book of Psalms provides numerous examples of this kind of "borrowing." One place to begin is Psalm 29. Many biblical scholars consider this psalm to be one of the oldest in the collection. The phrase "voice of the Lord" occurs seven times (29:3, 4, 5, 7, 8, 9). That is a metaphor for "thunder," which is particularly associated with Baal, who rides on the clouds of the thunderstorm (see Psalm 68:4, where Israel's God is also so pictured). At the end of Psalm 29, the Lord's enthronement over the floodwaters is celebrated (29:10), imagery that is reminiscent of Baal's victory over his challengers, particularly Yam the sea-god, and his enthronement over the Canaanite pantheon. Because of these suggestive parallels (and others having to do with the poetic style used, something that can only be recognized by looking at the Hebrew text in comparison with Ugaritic poetic texts), many consider Psalm 29 as probably a Canaanite hymn that was "borrowed" and transformed into a hymn of praise directed to the Lord God of Israel (see Dahood 1966, 175).

That the praise directed to a deity in one religious system can so easily be turned to the praise of a deity in another religion is most interesting. It suggests, correctly, that worshipers in a variety of religious traditions "feel" similarly with respect to the awe and devotion they find important to express to their god. Some of the images they use will no doubt be different because of local particularities (e.g., a nomadic group would find it difficult to use images comfortable to those of a settled agricultural community). But the emotions of religious devotion, the "heart seeing," are quite similar among adherents of the vast variety of religions found around the world.

Psalm 29 suggests yet another somewhat different, yet parallel, type of "borrowing." The psalm concludes with praises for the Lord, who is enthroned as "king forever" (29:10). As "king" the Lord was beseeched to "give strength to his people" and to "bless his people with peace" (29:11). In the eyes of the Mesopotamians of antiquity, such was the duty of earthly kings, and divine kingship—the responsibilities of God, so to speak—was held to the same standard.

In the Code of Hammurabi we read about the basic duties of the king, as enumerated at the beginning of the code: "Anum and Enlil [Mesopotamian deities] named me to promote the welfare of the people, me Hammurabi, the devout, god-fearing prince, to cause justice to prevail in the land, to destroy the wicked and the evil, that the strong might not oppress the weak" (Pritchard 1955, 164). Or again as found in the Ugaritic (Phoenician/Canaanite) Legend of King Keret, the king, due to illness, was thought no longer able to rule effectively. Thus his challenger chastised him:

> Thou [King Keret] hast let thy hand fall into mischief.
> Thou judgest not the cause of the widow,
>   Nor adjudicat'st the case of the wretched;
>   Driv'st not out them that prey on the poor;
> Feed'st not the fatherless before thee,
>   The widow behind thy back.
>   (Pritchard 1995, 149)

There are numerous passages in the Bible where the kings of Israel and the people are admonished for their failure to care properly for those in their charge. The language used is that of the standards applied to Mesopotamian kings. I cite but a few, first from Isaiah:

> Wash yourselves; make yourselves clean;
>   remove the evil of your doings from before my eyes;
> cease to to evil,
>   learn to do good;
> seek justice,
>   rescue the oppressed,
> defend the orphan,
>   plead for the widow.
>   (Isaiah 1:16–17)

Again, from Jeremiah:

> For if you truly amend your ways and your doings, if you truly act justly one with another, if you do not oppress the alien, the orphan, and the widow, or shed innocent blood in this place, and if you do not go after other gods to your own hurt, then I will dwell with you in this place, in the land that I gave of old to your ancestors forever and ever. (Jeremiah 7:5–7)

In Israel, the reason the king and the people were expected to pursue justice and care for the needy finally stemmed from the fact that such was the divine agenda. Thus Psalm 146 declares:

Happy are those whose help is in the God of Jacob,
  Whose hope is in the LORD their God,
Who made heaven and earth,
  the sea, and all that is in them;
who keeps faith forever;
who executes justice for the oppressed;
who gives food to the hungry.
The LORD sets the prisoners free;
  the LORD opens the eyes of the blind.
The LORD lifts up those who are bowed down;
  the Lord loves the righteous.
The LORD watches over the strangers;
  he upholds the orphan and the widow,
  but the way of the wicked he brings to ruin.
                                    (Psalm 146:5–9)

What is important to note here is that this "moral" instruction, while given a divine sanction in Israel, was not unique to ancient Israel. A similar code of behavior is found in a variety of texts that have been recovered from Israel's neighbors. Recognition of what was necessary to enable a community to function fairly and productively was not limited to Israel. Others held similar values, and in a number of instances the records preserved demonstrate that these values were hundreds of years old before Israel entered the scene. If we believe that God instructed Israel in the ways that they should live, and I for one do so believe, then it seems clear that God may well have instructed other, more-ancient peoples as well (cf. Romans 2:14–15). Our shared (borrowed?) values point in that direction.

Here is one further example of how Israel drew upon the wider culture to express theological conviction. In a number of places in the First (Old) Testament, the language of covenant is employed to describe Israel's relationship with God. Covenants were agreements common in the political and civil spheres of everyday life. Nations established treaties or covenants to define their relationships with others. Individuals fashioned promissory documents to describe civil agreements such as marriages or land transfers. Though many Christians (and perhaps Jews and Muslims as well) have by long custom come to understand the term "covenant" in a primarily religious, theological way, that was not the original nuance of the term at all. The language and forms of "covenant" were drawn from the "secular" sphere of life.

There are at least two types of covenantal terminology and style used in the First Testament. First, and most important for the overall theology of Israel, there is the covenant of obligation. This is the form of covenant that was established between God and Israel at Mount Sinai (see Exodus 19–24). The background for this form of covenant seems to be that of either the suzerainty treaties used among the Hittites (located mainly in what is now Turkey) during the late second millennium BCE or those of the Assyrians (located mainly in what is now Iraq, though their empire included all of the Fertile Crescent) in the seventh century BCE. In either instance, the dominant kings managed their empires by establishing treaties between themselves (the suzerains) and their subjects (vassals). The suzerain was "father" and the vassals were "sons" (and "brothers" between themselves). The suzerain established the treaty and stipulated the obligations that were imperative for the vassal to meet. In return, the vassal was assured protection from hostile neighbors or any invading forces. In the Old Testament the Ten Commandments (Exodus 20:1–17; Deuteronomy 5:6–21) are representative of the full set of stipulations given to Israel. The blessings and curses found in Deuteronomy 27–28, on the other hand, are examples of the obligations accepted by God.

The second form of covenant found in the Old Testament is what is called a "promissory covenant." It is fashioned after the royal land grants used by the Assyrian kings to reward particularly faithful service on the part of a royal subject. Land was given, and the grant was guaranteed by a covenantal document. No obligations were imposed by the monarch. This is the type of covenant that was granted to Abraham and Sarah (see Genesis 17) and, later, to David (see 2 Samuel 7). (For a more detailed discussion of the topic of covenant, see Hillers 1969; McCarthy 1972; March 2007.)

The point of this excursion into the social background of ancient Israel and the Bible is to underscore that there was an active interchange between the peoples living in Mesopotamia and along the eastern coast of the Mediterranean Sea in the second and first millennia BCE. During the centuries of biblical Israel's historical existence, the Israelites were relatively small in number and power. They won their share of battles with some of the smaller states around them, but not against the Mesopotamian empires or over Egypt. They were a minority and lived that way. They readily borrowed what was useful and then tweaked it to meet their particular need. In doing so, the writers of the Bible suggest to us readers of the Bible that some form of "pure" religion is not likely to come our way. Rather, and for this we should be thankful, the revelation of God comes to us through very human language, symbol, and mediation. God is at work through us and through those around us—insiders and outsiders—to guide us along God's way.

So far I have tried to establish the point that for many reasons—but particularly because of a tremendous increase in the diversity of the religious climate—the context, our context, for interpreting the Bible has changed. That does not mean that we should deny the particularity—even the, at times, harsh particularity of our histories—but we are in a position to point to other ways to understand our stories, ways imbedded within or beneath the primary narratives of our traditions. The implicit story of divine love should not be allowed to go unrecognized because there are those who prosper by selling "harsh texts." We owe more to our people than the somewhat simplistic "answers" that have for too long been advanced in the name of "religious authority." Our context challenges us to lead the way into a deeper appreciation of the implicit (and often explicit) inclusiveness of God's way preserved in the biblical traditions we cherish.

A new approach is in order. A new sensitivity and a reconsideration of our foundational documents are called for. For those of us in the business of interpreting the sacred texts of our traditions, it becomes imperative, it seems to me, to choose "generous texts" to inform our constituencies. There are many things in the Bible that my mother was never told about, and she deserved to be informed so that she could better understand what God is doing in our time. Let us continue our explorations.

Discussion Questions

1. In what ways does the church "borrow" metaphors from contemporary society to express its message for people who may not understand the ancient symbols? Have you experienced "heart

seeing"? When? What does the evidence of the Bible suggest concerning the merits of such "borrowing"?

2. What are some of the difficulties in using "king" language in our modern historical setting where monarchy is no longer common as a form of government? What duties of ancient kings were surprising to you? How can this imagery be translated?

3. What differences/similarities are there between the different kinds of covenant mentioned in the Bible? What can we learn from these covenants about our relationship with God? How can we translate these ancient symbols into modern language?

Chapter Eight

Surprising Strangers

*I*n 539 BCE a momentous change took place in Babylon! A *Persian,* Cyrus the Great, overpowered the Babylonian armies and put an end to the Babylonian Empire! This in itself was a mighty achievement. But what made it all the more noteworthy, from our point of view, was how Cyrus justified his actions. He claimed that he had been personally selected by *Marduk, Babylon's own protecting deity,* and directed to capture Marduk's city in order to restore the proper worship of Marduk. This shocker is recorded on the now-famous Cyrus Cylinder, which can be seen in the British Museum in London. But before we continue, a little background is in order.

From approximately 2500 BCE until 550 BCE, roughly two millennia, the area in the Middle East that we know as the Fertile Crescent was ruled from either Babylon or Nineveh. The primary territory of the Babylonian and Assyrian Empires stretched from Ur in the southeast (roughly where the current city of Basra, Iraq, is located, near the north end of the Persian Gulf) to the northwest into what is now Syria and clear to the Mediterranean Sea. Of course, the extended empires often included much more, depending upon the circumstances of the time, at their largest claiming all of what are now Syria, Lebanon, Jordan, Palestine, Israel, and parts of Egypt, Turkey, Saudi Arabia, and Iran.

The competition between Nineveh (Assyria), in the north on the Tigris River, and Babylon (Babylonia), in the south on the Euphrates River, was intense and ongoing with power shifting back and forth every couple of centuries, usually at the point of a sword. The culture that developed in the area across the years, however, was for all practical purposes one. The language throughout the region was essentially the same (a form of Semitic), a shared form of writing was developed (syllabic cuneiform), and the same basic pantheon of deities (though sometimes with different names for particular gods/goddesses) was assumed. The military might of both the Assyrians and the Babylonians was both feared and hated by those they conquered and ruled.

Toward the end of the seventh century BCE the power tipped to Babylon. Nebuchadnezzar II was the most powerful ruler of what we call the Neo-Babylonian Empire, reigning from 605 to 562 BCE. It was his armies that captured Jerusalem in 598. By his command much of Judah's leadership was taken into exile in Babylonia. Nebuchadnezzar's troops returned in 587, when Judah's King Zedekiah revolted. This time they destroyed the Temple in Jerusalem and tore down Jerusalem's walls. His son Amel-Marduk (Evil-merodach in the Bible: 2 Kings 25:27) succeeded him and reigned for two years (562–560 BCE). Then, after four years of unrest, Nabonidus (not of Nebuchadnezzar's dynasty, but still a Babylonian) took over and reigned from 556 to 539 BCE.

Cyrus the Great brought an end to the reign of Nabonidus. He captured Babylon in 538 BCE and assumed control. In the Cyrus Cylinder account, Nabonidus was chastised for failing to honor Marduk appropriately. What he actually did or did not do is lost to history. But Cyrus's response to the situation was dramatic and unprecedented. He instituted a new way of "doing empire." He recognized that the Babylonians had usually "taken captive" the deities as well as the people they conquered. Thus, to the numerous cities conquered by the Babylonians whose sanctuaries were in ruins, Cyrus returned "the images which (used) to live therein and established for them permanent sanctuaries. I (also) gathered all their (former) inhabitants and returned (to them) their habitations" (Pritchard 1955, 316). In other words, Cyrus adopted a policy of restoring destroyed temples and allowing the renewal of worship of the deities particular to those areas. This necessarily required, as well, allowing exiles to return to their original homelands. Thus, what we read about Cyrus in 2 Chronicles is perfectly in keeping with Cyrus's own words in the Cyrus Cylinder:

> Thus says King Cyrus of Persia: The LORD, the God of heaven, has given me all the kingdoms of the earth, and he has charged me to

build him a house at Jerusalem, which is in Judah. Whoever is among you of all his people, may the LORD his God be with him! Let him go up. (2 Chronicles 36:23; cf. Ezra 1:2–3)

So Cyrus made his proclamation and allowed the Judeans (and other ethnic groups) to return to their homelands.

What is somewhat even more surprising, however, is what the exilic Isaiah wrote about this Persian monarch at about the same time:

> Thus says the LORD, your Redeemer,
>   who formed you in the womb, . . .
>   who frustrates the omens of liars, . . .
>   who confirms the word of his servant, . . .
>   who says of Cyrus, "He is my shepherd,
>   and he shall carry out all my purpose." . . .
> Thus says the Lord to his anointed [messiah], to Cyrus,
>   whose right hand I have grasped
> to subdue nations before him
>   and strip kings of their robes,
> to open doors before him—
>   and the gates shall not be closed: . . .
> For the sake of my servant Jacob,
>   And Israel my chosen,
> I call you by your name,
>   I surname you, though you do not know me.
> I am the LORD, and there is no other;
>   besides me there is no god.
> I arm you, though you do not know me,
> so that they may know, from the rising of the sun
>   and from the west, that there is no one besides me;
>   I am the LORD, and there is no other.
> I form light and create darkness,
>   I make weal and create woe;
>   I the LORD do all these things.
>   (Isaiah 44:24–45:7)

Now that is a remarkable statement! The prophet announced that God was at work through a Persian who didn't even know who God was! Moreover, Isaiah called Cyrus God's *Messiah,* God's anointed one, selected to advance the divine purpose, against which no one would prevail. A "stranger" perhaps to Israel, but not to God; an "outsider" to the Judean exiles, who may not have had much understanding of what was happening on the international scene, but integral to God's purposes for Judah and the world.

There are a number of stories in the Bible about God's revelation of the divine will being made known in or through strangers. Three of them will make the point. Let's begin in the camp of a seminomad named Abraham, who with his wife, Sarah, and their family was encamped "by the oaks of Mamre," which was near the ancient (and modern) city of Hebron in Palestine (Genesis 18:1). Abraham was sitting in the shade of his tent, avoiding the heat of the day as best he could, when three men appeared (18:2–3). In accordance with the best etiquette of the Bedouin-like seminomad that he was, Abraham sprang to his feet and greeted the strangers. He insisted on their staying with him at least long enough for them to rest and receive nourishment (18:3–5). They agreed, and the meal was prepared and served, a feast of roasted meat, fresh bread, and all the "fixins" (18:6–8).

Now, the surprise in all this was at least twofold. First, Sarah was promised that she would conceive and bear a son, long after menopause had rendered that impossible for her (18:10–11). This is but one of a number of stories about barren or virgin women becoming pregnant by divine will (e.g., Rachel in Genesis 30:22–24; Hannah in 1 Samuel 1:19–20; Elizabeth in Luke 1:7–25; Mary in Luke 1:26–38). But second, in the course of the visit by these three strangers, the one who made the promise to Sarah is suddenly identified by the narrator of the story as "the LORD" (Genesis 18:10, 13–14). No one present at Abraham and Sarah's camp, including the two main characters, had any suspicion that God had somehow come near to them in the presence of the three travelers. The Lord only became known when the divine promise was made.

The sequel to this account finds Abraham going with the three visitors to Sodom to show them the way (Genesis 18:16). There again it was revealed that the Lord was present and intended to bring destruction on Sodom and Gomorrah (18:17–21). When it became clear to Abraham that he was dealing with the Lord, a remarkable exchange took place. In essence Abraham appealed to the divine sense of justice to spare Sodom if as few as ten righteous people could be found within it (18:22–32). The Lord granted Abraham's plea for mercy (though the subsequent account denies that there were even ten who were righteous in Sodom), and then Abraham and the Lord parted ways (18:33).

There is much to consider when reading this incredible account. How literally should we read it? Does God really walk around in the dust of this world somewhat in disguise (since God was not initially recognized)? Do such things still happen? Such a line of questions could continue for some time, but the very least we should understand from this story is that God can, has, probably will again, appear in our midst, often in the strangest and most unexpected ways, in and through the most unlikely of people.

Our next example is drawn from a book written hundreds of years later, indeed after the life, death, and resurrection of Jesus of Nazareth. The source is the New Testament book of Hebrews. In the thirteenth chapter an extraordinary statement is made in a most disarming way: "Do not neglect to show hospitality to strangers, for by doing that some have entertained angels without knowing it" (13:2). The hospitality of Abraham and Sarah at Mamre quite possibly provides the background for this admonition.

The charge to show hospitality is found in several different places in the Bible. Leviticus 19:34 and Deuteronomy 16:11–14 instruct Israel to deal hospitably with the aliens/strangers (among others) in the community since the people of Israel were once strangers themselves in the land of Egypt. Jesus demonstrated an act of hospitality when he washed the feet of his disciples (John 13:1–20). Paul instructed the Christians in Rome to "extend hospitality to strangers" (Romans 12:13; see also 1 Peter 4:9). And a necessary qualification for becoming a bishop was to be hospitable (1 Timothy 3:2; Titus 1:8).

What sets the admonition in Hebrews apart is the explanation that sometimes strangers may actually be "angels" (divine messengers) who provide the occasion for God to enter the situation. As with Abraham and Sarah, who at first did not recognize God's presence, their willingness to show proper hospitality to the travelers enabled them to make a connection that they presumably would have missed otherwise. For the writer of Hebrews to share this exhortation is especially remarkable since the book as a whole seems to present a very "exclusive" understanding of God's work with humankind. How can this writer really entertain the notion that God might visit the community in the form of strangers/angels?

The writer of Hebrews presents an extended, well-articulated argument that asserts the legitimacy of the Christian movement. The church has a special place in God's providential plan, which is demonstrated by the superiority of Christ over against the angels (Hebrews 1:5–14), the work of Christ over against that of Moses (3:1–19), the priesthood of Christ over against the Temple priesthood (4:14–16), the new covenant mediated by Christ over against the former covenant established at Sinai (8:1–13), and the finality of Christ's once-for-all sacrifice for the forgiveness of sin over against the need to offer sacrifices repeatedly (9:23–10:18). Those who follow Jesus are assured of the effectiveness of God's love for them!

Now it is at this point that we must listen carefully for what the writer of Hebrews was trying to communicate. For a very long time the book of Hebrews has been heard as dismissing Israel as the people of God and installing the church in its place. The book of Hebrews has been one of the sources, if not the primary source, in the New Testament for the doctrine of supersessionism, the belief that the church has replaced Israel as the people of God. But the writer of Hebrews, I believe, had something else in mind.

The book was clearly intended to encourage the Christians to whom it was initially addressed to stand firm in the midst of some kind of difficult situation. The writer was trying to inspire and/or renew their zeal for the faith (Hebrews 5:11–14; 6:9–12; 12:7–12). Earlier times of suffering and persecution were recalled (10:32–34). Then we read the words:

> Do not, therefore, abandon that confidence of yours; it brings great reward. For you need endurance, so that when you have done the will of God, you may receive what was promised.
>
> For yet "in a very little while,
>   the one who is coming will come and will not delay;
> but my righteous one will live by faith;
>   My soul takes no pleasure in anyone who shrinks back."
>
> But we are not among those who shrink back and so are lost, but among those who have faith and so are saved. (10:35–39)

The people were warned strongly against apostasy (12:14–29) and enjoined to resist those who were apparently trying to impose upon them "regulations about food," among other things (13:9).

The letter of Hebrews is a long exhortation to trust in God's abiding care. There is not so much concern about how non-Christians are related to God or with how they are to understand their relationship. Rather, it was written toward the end of the first century of the Common Era, as the church and the synagogue were slowly separating from one another. As the tensions rose and some of the Christian flock began to consider returning to their former understanding of their relationship with God, the question that the audience was asking was whether they were loved by God as much as the Jews were claimed as God's people. And the answer was a resounding "Yes!" The book of Hebrews does not provide us as a treatise on non-Christian religions. Rather, it offers a renewed call to committed discipleship. The showing of hospitality is one measure of that commitment, and it may well become an occasion for unexpectedly meeting God.

The third biblical example of the way that God can be seen in and/or through those whom we view as strangers and outsiders is found in the Gospel of Matthew in a very dramatic passage. Jesus is presented toward the end of his ministry as speaking about the coming reign of God. The disciples were urged to be prepared (Matthew 25:1–13) and to serve as trustworthy, productive stewards (25:14–30). Then, the final judgment by God, when the sheep would be separated from the goats, was described. And here is where the dramatic surprise is found. Jesus described the scene. All the nations would stand before him:

> Then the king will say to those at his right hand, "Come, you that are blessed by my Father, inherit the kingdom prepared for you from the foundation of the world; for I was hungry and you gave me food, I was thirsty and you gave me something to drink, I was a stranger and you welcomed me, I was naked and you gave me clothing, I was sick and you took care of me, I was in prison and you visited me." Then the righteous will answer him, "Lord, when was it that we saw you hungry and gave you food, or thirsty and gave you something to drink? And when was it that we saw you a stranger and welcomed you, or naked and gave you clothing? And when was it that we saw

you sick or in prison and visited you?" And the king will answer them, "Truly I tell you, just as you did it to one of the least of these who are members of my family [literally, the Greek reads "brothers"], you did it to me." (25:34–40; cf. 25:45)

The surprise in this statement is at least twofold. First, the standard of acceptability was announced to all the nations, not only to the followers of Jesus. God's expectations for proper behavior among the peoples of the world extended to all and not only to Israel and/or the church. Second, God was to be seen in the faces of those who were in great need. As people reached out to the hungry, thirsty, and ill, God was encountered. In the form of prisoners and strangers, God was near at hand. No doctrinal test or membership requirements had to be met. God was to be met in ministering to those who were in need. Acts of hospitality were the surest avenue to God.

In the various biblical stories that we have briefly considered, God was pictured as meeting humankind in unexpected ways, often in the form of a stranger. The powerful, such as Cyrus the Great, and the poor and helpless, including the ill and imprisoned, were agents through whom the person of God was to be recognized and the work of God carried forward. Strangers who unexpectedly appeared at the door were to be offered hospitality because God might well be present in the person of such strangers. God has not been limited to working only through the recognized channels. God moves mysteriously, at times engaging human beings in unexpected ways. Two of Jesus' disciples discovered this on the road to Emmaus (see Luke 24:13–35).

When we interact with those outside our usual circle, outside our congregation, or even outside our religious tradition, we are taking a risk. They may not respond positively if at all. They may consider us negatively, as representative of a tradition whose adherents have too often been insensitive, insincere, and even abusive. Nonetheless, the mysterious God whom we have met in Jesus of Nazareth will not be confined to our categories or limited by our perceptions. Thus we do well to engage others in a spirit of hospitality. In so doing we may well "entertain angels," have our eyes opened and our hearts quickened, and meet God in the process.

Discussion Questions

1. How does the story about Abraham, Sarah, and the visitors shift back and forth from seemingly literal to clearly figurative language? What can we learn from this in terms of our own religious language?
2. What does the book of Hebrews tell us about hospitality, perseverance, and caring for one another? How might the contemporary church benefit from listening carefully to these teachings?
3. How is God pictured as a stranger or visitor in Genesis, Hebrews, and Matthew? In what ways does God surprise us now by meeting us in unsuspected places and through the "least" of these? What are we to learn about "ministering" from these passages?

PART 3

A New Mission

Learning and Sharing

Chapter 9

Words Matter

*I*n the December 26, 2006, issue of *The Christian Century,* Amy-Jill Levine wrote an insightful article titled "Misusing Jesus." Professor Levine is a Jew who teaches New Testament at Vanderbilt Divinity School. Her article was adapted from her longer work *The Misunderstood Jew* (2006). In her article Levine enumerated a number of ways that Christians purposefully or ignorantly misrepresent or misunderstand the implications of the fact that Jesus was a Jew. In introducing her topic, Levine penned the following, devastatingly accurate critique that speaks directly to the point:

> The problem is more than one of silence. In the popular Christian imagination, Jesus still remains defined, incorrectly and unfortunately, as "against" the Law, or at least against how it was understood at the time; as "against" the Temple as an institution and not simply against its first-century leadership; as "against" the people Israel but in favor of the gentiles.

In such a distorted view of who Jesus really was, Levine continues:

> Jesus becomes the rebel who, unlike every other Jew, practices social justice. He is the only one to speak with women; he is the only one who teaches nonviolent responses to oppression; he is the only one who cares about the "poor and the marginalized" (that phrase becomes a litany in some Christian circles). Judaism becomes in such discourse a negative foil: whatever Jesus stands for, Judaism isn't it; whatever Jesus is against, Judaism epitomizes the category. (20)

Each of the categories Levine discusses represents an area where Christians need to do a much better job of contextualizing the text for our congregants, for ourselves! Her critique is well worth your review. We are in danger of bearing false witness!

One place to begin is with some of the language we use. I do not mean some of the scandalous slang expressions I grew up with, such as "He tried to Jew me down," "She/he is such a Pharisee," and so forth; these hateful slurs have no place in anyone's speech! Here, I want to address another dimension of reference that may not be as immediately critical but is nonetheless important, particularly as a reminder of our new circumstance.

Some second-century Christians inadvertently created a problem for contemporary Christians by coining a term. Drawing on references to new and old "covenants" ("testaments" in Latin), they began to refer to the Bible that they shared with second-century Jews as the "Old Testament" in distinction from an emerging body of materials that came to be known as the "New Testament." Literarily the term "Old Testament" did not appear until around 180 CE.

Although there were perhaps justifiable reasons for this terminology in the second century, in contemporary North American culture the term "Old Testament" creates a problem. First, "old," for many in our cultural situation, signifies something that is near or at the end of its usefulness, like old clothes or an old car or an old body, for that matter. Only a few prefer "old movies" or "old homes." Second, and more important, for some Christians, because of their obvious connection with the "Old Testament," the Jews are also considered as of little value. Like all things "old," the Jews and "their Bible" are probably best left behind. Such was the line of reasoning that some used in developing policy for the Third Reich, Nazi Germany.

To try to correct these misunderstandings, many people in biblical studies, at least, use the term "Hebrew Bible" to refer to the Old Testament. From my point of view, however, that term is not totally satisfactory. The literature to which the term is applied is not all Hebrew (some of it is in Aramaic), and it also sets up a possible parallel for the "New Testament" being labeled the Greek Bible, which is certainly inaccurate. What's more, for some Christian churches, like the Presbyterian Church (U.S.A.), their Book of Order and Confessions require that the term "Old Testament" be retained. This term is part of their confessional vocabulary.

Personally, I prefer to use the terms the "First Testament" and the "Second Testament." That is neutral language that does not in itself claim too little or too much. I have no intention to cease use of the term "Old Testament," but "First Testament" has become a frequent part of my liturgical and scholarly vocabulary. (I recently heard a Jewish rabbi friend of mine quip that OT actually means "Only Testament.")

While we are messing with traditional language, let's also challenge the nomenclature for referencing time: AD = anno Domini, "the year of our Lord" (unless you are in the military, and then you might think "Active Duty") and BC = before Christ (unless you are a Canadian, and you might think British Columbia). To be sure the abbreviations BC/AD have been around for a good while, and "everybody uses them," or so we are told.

So far as I know, however, that was not true for the first five hundred years or so of the Christian movement. A monk named Dionysius Exiguus, sometime in the 500s of the Common Era, was the first to use these terms to designate time categories. But not until nearly nine hundred years later, by around 1400, did the BC/AD system come into wide use in Europe. Clearly, this terminology is not rooted in divine revelation! Nor was it, or is it, used worldwide. Christians created it in a world where they were dominant, primarily in the Western world. While Jews and Muslims (and others) largely ignored it, at least so far as religious chronology was concerned, there was no one to question it or challenge it, so it became "the standard."

But now there are those who want to question this arbitrary chronological nomenclature, and I think we should. Indeed, among biblical scholars, BCE (before the Common Era) and CE (Common Era) are now used routinely. This is not a plot to get rid of Jesus, no matter what some of the conspiracy theorists among us may say. Rather, the scholarly community has found that this terminology effectively designates events before the time of Jesus and after Jesus without the religious imperialism of the "traditional" lingo. Thus BCE and CE are ever more frequently being used in the commentaries and in the journal articles we all use, so we had best explain it to everyday Christians for whom it might seem strange, people like my mother.

There is no reason for our various constituencies to get all worked up. The point is simply to desist from using terminology that is needlessly offensive to some. The wider challenge is to educate our people about the origins of other religious traditions and to the fact that most of them significantly predate Christianity. For well over two billion non-Christians in our world, Jesus' appearance is not the defining event in history. For me, this change in terminology represents honest sensitivity to the fact that we no longer live in the "Middle Ages."

We are beginning to come to grips with the fact that Jews and Christians share a common history before and after Jesus, but the pre-Jesus origin of most of the other classical religions has something more to suggest to us about God's work beyond our context. And the First Testament provides some guidance. Amos, some eight hundred years before Jesus, gave the ancient Israelites a hint when he said on behalf of God: "Are you not like the Ethiopians to me, O people of Israel? says the LORD. Did I not bring Israel up from the land of Egypt, and the Philistines from Caphtor and the Arameans from Kir?" (Amos 9:7). God has never been limited to the particular task of engaging only Israel or only the church! God's world is much larger!

Christian leaders, frankly, have a serious language problem that must be faced. As presently translated, there are some texts in the Second Testament that are, or at least appear to be, blatantly anti-Jewish. We are first of all concerned with a misrepresentation of Jews and Judaism, but the attitudes prompted by some of these texts are not limited to perceptions of Jews alone. They spill over to poison our understanding of other religious traditions as well.

There are some ways to deal with some of these passages relatively simply. We need to remember the context of the early Jesus movement. Jesus himself was a Jew, and so were his first followers. Judaism as a religion, as we know it, had not developed in the time of Jesus and would not until sometime in the middle of the second century CE. There was great diversity among those who had common roots in the literary traditions that sometime in the early second century CE came to be called the Bible. No one group could claim the title of "Jewish," at least not to the exclusion of others. So, when we read in English translations of the Bible the terms "Jew" or "Jews," we will do well to interpret the language as "a certain Jew" or "some Jews." Better yet, as noted in chapter 2, we might more accurately reflect the original texts if we would use terms like "the Judeans" or "the Galileans." All of the Jews did not reject Jesus; only some of the Jews did so. Only some of the Jewish leaders, only some of the Pharisees, were hostile toward the Jew named Jesus. We need to stress this with our people, even at the risk of sounding pedantic.

Second, we do well to remind our people over and over that Jesus was a Jew of his own time. He knew and observed Jewish tradition. He taught little (if anything) that had not already been articulated in Jewish tradition. For him to instruct his disciples to love one another was not a radically new teaching. Yet we sometimes, too often I suspect, try to present Jesus' teachings as in some manner brand new, unique, in sharp contrast to the teachings of others of his time. We do this, at times, in an attempt to demonstrate that Christian views are inherently superior to those of Jews, and thus to be accepted. At other times, we do so out of ignorance of Jewish tradition. We may well find that Jesus' teachings claim and challenge *us* more than those of any other in the world, but we should not "explain" or try to "prove" our choice on the basis of the supposed uniqueness or the more "spiritual" quality of our traditions.

More difficult to deal with are some passages in the Pauline Letters where the term "Jew" does not actually refer to some one who is "Jewish." What do I mean? Well, much of the controversy found in Paul's Letters seems to have been intra-Christian, a debate among different factions within the early church. Some Christians called other Christians "Jews" (we now use the term "Judaizers") to belittle or deny the legitimacy of their insistence on the necessity of circumcision and Sabbath keeping. Some of these "Judaizers" may have been born Jewish, but most, apparently, were Gentile converts to Christianity who thought Jewish custom was essential for Christian faithfulness.

There was a genuine debate in the early church between these various camps. In fact, it lasted well into the second century of the Christian movement. This difficulty is remembered explicitly in the New Testament in the books of Acts and Galatians, where controversy between Peter and Paul is recounted (see Acts 10–15; Galatians 2:4–5). For Paul, the point at issue was how Gentile converts to the church were to be received and treated. For example, Paul wanted his Gentile converts released from any obligation to follow the Jewish custom of circumcision. Paul was certain that Gentiles did not have to become circumcised just because Jews traditionally were circumcised. On this he was adamant.

But there were other issues where Paul was willing to compromise. When it came to issues concerning Jewish food laws, for instance, he was less dogmatic. With respect to whether to eat certain foods or not, Paul counseled Gentile Christians to respect the sensitivities of others. The people of the ancient world did not actually eat much meat. When they did so, it was often from animals that had been sacrificed to a god or goddess. (This was also true for Jews. Their primary source for meat, so long as the Temple stood in Jerusalem, was from sacrificed animals.) Thus, to eat the meat of sacrificed animals could be seen as participating in the worship of "deities" to whom the animal had first been offered. This, it seemed to some, was tantamount to idolatry, which was strongly prohibited. In light of this, Paul reasoned, it was better for people to abstain from eating food that had possibly been offered to idols, not because he believed the food itself was contaminated, but because there was no need in unnecessarily offending either Jews who had become Christians or Gentile Christian "Judaizers" who might misunderstand. What is especially important to note here is that most of this discussion is directed within Paul's community, within the Christian movement, to Christians who wanted to act like Jews rather than to actual Jews. It was a word to "insiders," not "outsiders."

When we see the term "Jew" in the Pauline Letters, it is all too easy to jump immediately to the twenty-first century and equate the people in question with Jews as we know them today. Such a jump totally disregards the context out of which these texts came. Many of the New Testament "anti-Jewish" writings were not actually addressed to Jews or even about Jews. They were part of a literature struggling with the issue of "Judaizing." To help casual readers of these texts contextualize them properly is not easy, but it is an effort we need to make.

Scripture does not reflect very much upon all of those people who stand beyond the category "Jew" or "Christian," but there are statements about "Gentiles" in relation to "Jews" suggesting that God is quite inclusive toward the "others." I have already noted Amos, and there are more. The book of Jonah celebrates the repentance—not the conversion, it should be noted (Jonah 3:6–10)—and deliverance of the Ninevites, traditional and real enemies of Israel and Judah, because of the gracious mercy of God. The book of Job, with an Edomite (another traditional enemy) as the major figure, articulates a profound understanding of the extent of God's work. God even speaks though the donkey of a non-Israelite Mesopotamian named Balaam! (Numbers 22:22–30). While God does require of us exclusive allegiance, that does not automatically define or limit God's relationship to others. But it is worth asking a simple question: "Why should we Christians think for a minute that God does not redemptively love others as God has loved us?"

Respectful, honest language with respect to Jews and all those "others" is what I am urging Christians to adopt. But there is something else at stake as well in what we have just been considering: a better understanding of what the Bible meant and means. Assuming old lines of exclusivistic interpretation (that only Christians are really important before God) has led to a perversion of the Bible, especially of the New Testament. To say it once more, the Second Testament (and the First, for that matter) was written within a community that represented a very small fraction of the population of the Roman Empire during the first two centuries of the Common Era. The churches in Corinth and in Ephesus, for instance, were very, very small in terms of the numbers of those cities overall. The writers of the Second Testament were primarily writing to offer encouragement and instruction to enable the early Christians to survive in the midst of an extraordinarily diverse environment, religiously, socially, and ethnically.

What we need to do, then, is to keep that context in mind when we read the Bible. It was written by "insiders" for "insiders," not "insiders" against "outsiders." The stirring words of 1 Peter 2:9 offer a case in point:

> But you are a chosen race, a royal priesthood, a holy nation, God's own people, in order that you may proclaim the mighty acts of him who called you out of darkness into his marvelous light.

By claiming images and metaphors from the First Testament that helped to describe ancient Israel, the author urged the members of several small, struggling congregations located in Asia Minor (currently Turkey) to faithfulness. The people were not told that they alone counted before God, but they were assured, strongly assured, that *they did count*! They were a distinct minority within the dominant society, but they were very important to God.

The bottom line? Nowhere is it said that God didn't or doesn't care for others and doesn't have relationships with non-Christians or non-Jews as well. One might debate how that might be possible, but the text itself doesn't go there, and in my opinion we shouldn't either. We need to open our eyes and marvel in our hearts that God's love is as deep and wide as the ocean. We, no more than my mom, need try to "defend" or "restrict" God.

Discussion Questions

1. Why is language important in talking about God and about our relationships with people of other religions? What are the difficulties of trying to change long-standing terminology concerning the Testaments or calendar? Why should we even try?

2. How do contemporary translations of the Bible complicate the way we are to understand biblical terminology referring to persons living in Judea—Judeans—by often rendering the term as "Jews"? What are some of the alternatives?

3. How does the Bible picture God relating to peoples other than Israel or the church? What does that suggest about the rather common exclusivist assumptions often expressed among Christians about others of a different faith? What might be done to alter this misconception?

Chapter 10

"These and These"

Columnist David Brooks, in a piece entitled "Lessons from U.N. Week" in the *New York Times* on September 11, 2006, drew attention to several lessons to be learned as we consider the tragic events of 9/11/01. One was this:

> A huge gap is emerging between the way ordinary Americans see the Arab world and the way members of the political, media and intellectual elites see it.
>
> Elite debate is restrained by a series of enlightened attitudes that amount to a code of political correctness: be tolerant of cultural differences, seek to understand the responses of people who feel oppressed, don't judge groups, never criticize somebody else's religion.
>
> As anybody who has traveled around the country or listened to talk radio of left, right and center knows, these genteel manners do not inhibit the masses. Millions of Americans think the pope asked exactly the right questions [in his lecture concerning Islam]: Does the Muslim God accord with the categories of reason? Are Muslims trying to spread their religion with the sword?
>
> These Americans don't believe they should lower their standards of tolerable behavior merely for the sake of multicultural politeness, and they are growing ever more disgusted with commentators and leaders who are totally divorced from the reality they see on TV every night.

In the February 4, 2008, issue of *Newsweek*, George Weigel wrote this:

That is what we are fighting; jihadism, the religiously inspired ideology which teaches that it is every Muslim's duty to use any means necessary to compel the world's submission to Islam. That most of the world's Muslims do not accept this definition of the demands of their faith is true—and beside the point. The jihadists believe this. That is why they are the enemy of their fellow Muslims and the rest of the world. For decades, an internal Islamic civil war, born of Islam's difficult encounter with modernity, has been fought over such key modern political ideas as religious toleration and the separation of religious and political authority in a just state. That intra-Islamic struggle now engages the rest of humanity. . . .

The jihadist merchants of death must be defeated morally as well as militarily. Doing so offers the American people the opportunity for national self-renewal and the chance to defend the cause of human dignity throughout the world. The stakes—the future of freedom—are very high indeed. It's past time for those who would lead us to acknowledge that. (49)

Weigel's essay is adapted from his book *Faith, Reason, and the War against Jihadism* (2007).

Steven Erlanger, a reporter for the *New York Times,* noted the insulting, inciting language of the Hamas leadership in Gaza, which poisons the present climate and is producing a whole new generation of children taught suspicion and hate. In his April 1, 2008, story he wrote:

At Al Omari mosque, the imam cursed the Jews and the "Crusaders," or Christians, and the Danes, for reprinting cartoons of the Prophet Muhammad. He referred to Jews as "the brothers of apes and pigs," while the Hamas television station, Al Aksa, praises suicide bombings and holy war until Palestine is free of Jewish control. . . .

Hamas's grip on Gaza matters, but what may matter more in the long run is its control over propaganda and education there, breeding longer-term problems for Israel, for peace. No matter what Israeli and Palestinian negotiators agree upon, there is concern here that the attitudes being instilled will make a sustainable peace extremely difficult. (1)

David Brooks, George Weigel, and Steven Erlanger reflect different issues posed by the rise of militants, particularly Islamic militants, in the past twenty-five years, difficult issues that we all must address. Many are at a loss when considering Islam as a religion: is it a religion of peace and mercy, or a religion of war and domination? Do we fight jihadism as a political threat or a religious heresy? Is our Christian concern basically to protect Western ideals of toleration and the separation of religion and state, or is ours more of a theological question concerning how we are to relate to the adherents of other traditions?

These questions are not idle concerns. Freedom to exercise one's beliefs, whether political or religious, is a fundamental value that most Americans cherish. Yet in some ways the tradition of exclusivism, taught in many versions of Christianity, is as hostile (at least theoretically speaking) to the freedoms we cherish as is the exclusivism of the jihadists. So, from my point of view, one important issue that needs to be addressed is the theological one: Is there only one valid way to know and relate to God?

While Muslims may rightly be a preoccupation of the American public these days, there is a wide variety of religious and ethnic experience that seems "threateningly other" to many Americans, to many Christians. Perhaps more than at any other time in my life, I am encountering widespread expressions of xenophobia, the fear and/or disdain of those we consider "strangers" or "foreigners." Whether "they" are from south of our borders or from the Middle East, many Americans are forming opinions about "them" that may prove to be disastrous for all of us. I think we need to open our eyes and listen with our hearts to this emerging reality and to the danger that the fear and/or disdain of others poses if we leave the problem unacknowledged or unchallenged. This is now part of our context, a significant part. We are in a new situation, politically to be sure, but also theologically speaking.

At least three "facts" will affect the work of Christian theology for some time. First, North American and European Christians are declining in terms of "market share." We no longer are in the majority, not in the wider world nor in many of our local communities. Second, Christian theology, with respect to people of other religions, has for nearly fifteen hundred years been basically "exclusive." This I have tried to exemplify by considering our thinking concerning Jews and Judaism, but the same "exclusivism" has guided our relationships with others as well. Convert them, kill them, or ignore them, but certainly don't consider them as bearers of divine grace! Third, one "fact" seems to contradict some of what both Brooks and Weigel have written: some North American Christians are interacting more and more with people of other religions and are finding them engaging and honorable people. They know Sikhs and Muslims and Buddhists, firsthand in some instances, and find that those they know personally are good people who do not fit into the theological slot that the church for centuries has wanted to put them in.

The time is right for the church to reconsider its exclusivist position. The experience of Christians around the world suggests that it is imperative for us to learn how to live with one another not only with tolerance but also with appreciation. As we go about this work, we do well to recognize that alternative religious sensibilities are real and inevitable and, I believe, a part of the divine agenda for our time.

I recently saw a production of Aaron Posner's 1999 dramatic adaptation of Chaim Potok's classic novel *The Chosen* (1967). The play depicts the contrasting dynamics of a liberal Jewish professor and an orthodox Jewish rabbi with their respective sons. Each of these fathers was well versed in the Jewish tradition, but they held diametrically opposite views on the critical issue of Zionism, a burning issue among Jews in 1967 and yet today.

The play concluded with the two portrayed fathers diligently working to prepare statements of their theological/political convictions, and then the playwright presented them on opposite sides of the stage, reading their respective work to their followers. As the strident voices of the pro-Zionist professor and the anti-Zionist rabbi gave voice to their deep disagreement, a narrator concluded the scene and the play by recalling the famous passage in the Babylonian Talmud that settled a severe disagreement between the schools of Hillel and Shammai. The Talmud reported that a voice from heaven was heard saying, "These and these are the words of the living God, but the halakah is according to Hillel."

Both views were true, but that of Hillel was preferred. Why? The Talmud answered: because when Hillel used to speak, . . . he would always begin by mentioning Shammai's position first. He never taught Torah while pretending to possess the unique truth, but while admitting that two opinions might have plausibility and meaning. Yes, "these and these" are the words of the living God" (Talmud *Eruvin* 13b). This is an important position to adopt as we work with our people to understand our new context. There may be—in fact there probably are—multiple "truths" rather than one single "truth," at least on the human level.

This, of course, is not the way the church has viewed such matters for some centuries. But now we are in a new context. Professor John Pawlikowski, a highly respected Roman Catholic scholar (of the Catholic Theological Union, Chicago), has suggested that we must develop what he calls "a theology of religious pluralism." As he puts it:

A theology of religious pluralism might allow us to say we have more than others but never could it permit us to say we have a hold on all significant religious insight. This does not mean that each religious tradition is incapable of providing salvation for its adherents. What we need to recognize is that all of us are saved in our incompleteness. Along with Paul Tillich, I believe the theology of religious pluralism requires some notion of an ongoing revelatory process. I also acknowledge with Tillich that there may be a central event or events in the history of revelation. But "central" in my judgment need not imply exclusivity. As a Christian I would at least posit *both* Sinai and the Easter Event as equally central, and I would be open to a possible expansion of the list. Also, calling a revelatory event central does not in my mind automatically connote "completeness." A central event need not make all other revelatory experiences secondary and by implication of lesser value. But this has been precisely the problem with the way Christianity has usually presented its notion of the centrality of the Christ Event. (1994, 49)

Cynthia Campbell has expressed a complementary understanding in her volume *A Multitude of Blessings*:

God's providence has brought us to this time and this place—as Christians in a multifaith world. Perhaps the continuing vitality of the many world religions is part of God's way of relating to and caring for all of God's human community. . . . Perhaps truth about God and human life resides in us *and at the same time* in other traditions, because God is surely bigger than any one way of understanding and experiencing God. (101)

Christians have felt it necessary to understand their uniqueness as followers of Jesus Christ as requiring the negation of the distinctive viability of those of other commitments. In defining ourselves, we too often have done so by denying others. Our new context requires that we reconsider our theology as well as the way we interpret the Bible. Some of this work should be done and is being done among scholars and at the national level of several Christian denominations, but the real test will be at the level of the local congregation and presbytery.

The narrow-mindedness of some gets in the way of constructive theological reflection and beneficial religious practice. The insistence on maintaining theological propositions primarily on the grounds that this is the way Christian theology has in the past been articulated is not helpful nor, in my opinion, faithful to the One who is challenging us to a new level of obedience and service.

Christians are not alone in the practice of intolerance or uncritical preoccupation with tradition. The adherents of other religions at times can be just as closed minded and resistant to change as are Christians at times. Akbar S. Ahmed, one of the leading scholars in the world on contemporary Islam, and the current occupant of the Ibn Khaldun Chair of Islamic Studies at the American University in Washington, DC, has recently written a volume entitled *Journey into Islam: The Crisis of Globalization*. In this book Ahmed describes three models or interpretations of Islam that are followed by various communities of Muslims around the world. Ahmed is well aware of and accurately describes the spread of one interpretation of Islam, Deoband, a doctrinaire form that is orthodox in its understanding of Islam and exclusive in its perspective. The name derives from the "preeminent *madrassah,* or religious educational center, of South Asian Islam. . . . Like the better-known Wahhabi movement in the Arab world, it stands for assertive action in defending, preserving, and transmitting Islamic tradition and identity" (1). Deoband has produced communities that are essentially isolated from other Muslims and from adherents of other religions as well. It has become dominant in some places and is the form of Islam that is getting most of the press in the West since the events of 9/11.

But Ahmed also discusses two other forms of Islam, each quite different from the Deoband model. Sufism is a rather mystical expression of Islam that stresses the oneness of humankind and strives for cooperation among the peoples of all religions. It attracts a small but important following. Its disciples have been involved in interfaith sharing for many years. Ahmed refers to this form of Islam as the

"Ajmer" model because the shrine of one of its most esteemed leaders is in Ajmer, India (33–35).

The third of Ahmed's models he names "Aligarh," after another city in India where adherents to this understanding are found. It is a socially progressive, modernist approach that during the past century or so has been the choice of many intellectuals and educational leaders in the Muslim world. There is openness to others and the intention of using reason to fashion public policy. As Ahmed puts it, "Whether they are devout or more secular Muslims, followers of Aligarh share the desire to engage with modern ideas while preserving what to them is essential to Islam" (37).

Ahmed also offers comments on the interaction among the diverse expressions of the Muslim world he has described:

> Ajmer followers, for example, think Deobandis are too critical of other faiths and too preoccupied with opposing mysticism, while they find Aligarh followers too concerned with the material world. For their part, the followers of Deoband would consider those of Ajmer guilty of innovation and close to heresy and those of Aligarh far too secular and too influenced by the West. The Aligarh group would perceive Ajmer as backward and would dismiss Deoband as little more than a rabble of ignorant clerics, country bumpkins, and benighted rustics. (37)

The point of all of this is to help educate non-Muslims about the complexity of Islam, a diversity that is far more complex than the Shia-Sunni division that is only beginning to be recognized in the West. Further, Ahmed acknowledges the clash between the Muslim world and the West. He sees it as in part a continuation of the failed policy to divide the Muslim world by isolating groups the West finds unacceptable. This, in part, has led to a very widespread negative perception of the West, which is found in almost all parts of the Muslim world. Unless and until that basic mistrust is eliminated, any form of rapprochement will be extremely difficult. Nonetheless, Ahmed believes that the situation can be changed through contact, dialogue, and interaction by persons on various sides of the divide willing to try for a new understanding.

As we try to understand Islam and our relation with Muslims around the world, we will also do well to remember the comments concerning Islam by Jared Diamond in his best-selling book *Guns, Germs, and Steel*:

> Nowadays, Islamic societies in the Middle East are relatively conservative and not at the forefront of technology. But medieval Islam in the same region was technologically advanced and open to innovation. It achieved far higher literacy rates than contemporary Europe; it assimilated the legacy of classical Greek civilization to such a degree that many classical Greek books are now known to us only through Arabic copies; it invented or elaborated windmills, tidal mills, trigonometry, and lateen sails; it made major advances in metallurgy, mechanical and chemical engineering, and irrigation methods; and it adopted paper and gunpowder from China and transmitted them to Europe. In the Middle Ages the flow of technology was overwhelmingly from Islam to Europe, rather than from Europe to Islam as it is today. Only after around A.D. 1500 did the net direction of flow begin to reverse. (1997, 253)

Whatever we may find disturbing about contemporary Islam must be held in perspective. As Akbar Ahmed and Jared Diamond remind us, we are often reacting to one expression of Islamic religion while being quite ignorant of what has been and is now a quite different understanding shared by Muslims in many parts of the world.

I cannot change anyone, particularly those of other religious convictions. But I can call other Christians to a careful review of how we have understood and expressed our understanding of others and of divine grace. The kind of honest sharing that Ahmed calls for is possible. But for Christians to participate productively in such an exchange, I am convinced that we need to do some hard theological work on the matter of the "others" and God's relationship with them. For too long we have allowed former teaching on this matter to dictate our response. It is time to challenge doctrine that has separated us from others and to work with others to bridge the chasms that we have built between ourselves and others.

I am trying to challenge you and myself to explore and create new methods of biblical interpretation and theological interpretation. We who have thought of ourselves as being the "majority" are certainly no longer that as measured on the world map. That is our reality. Using the model of contextual interpretation developed by various racial and ethnic minorities, though modifying it somewhat, I am suggesting that we need to take our present social context, as well as the contexts from which the Bible and some of our long-held doctrines emerged, and reexamine who we are.

I believe that God is doing new things. We are not the victims of an inept divine strategy that has caused the multiplication of religious traditions across our world. No, look! Listen! The rich tapestry of religious tradition that we are beginning to encounter firsthand is God's gift to us, intended to help us better understand God's graciousness. Whether we open our eyes and listen with our hearts, however, is up to us, but my mom deserves better than she formerly received.

Discussion Questions

1. What are some of the ways "jihadism" has influenced the way we tend to think of Muslims today? How does this relate to the way other "foreigners" are perceived? What are some ways that the church might approach the various questions raised by this new circumstance?
2. How does the reality of religious pluralism affect the way other religions and their adherents should be viewed? What is gained or lost by insisting that there can be only one "truth"? How does your own experience of others of different traditions inform your thinking on these issues?
3. What are some of the varieties that exist within Islam? How can we learn more about them? What are some of the positive and negative contributions that Muslims have made and continue to make?

Chapter Eleven

Work to Do

*I*n Yann Martel's widely read novel *Life of Pi,* the hero is Piscine Molitor Patel, his name shortened to Pi for one obvious reason. "Piscine" is a name that adolescent boys can twist in too many directions. Pi is a delightful character, curious about life in general and religions (all religions) in particular. Pi was born a Hindu and cherished Hindu tradition and practice. But he also pursued an understanding of Christianity and Islam and thought of himself as a Hindu Christian Muslim. Pi saw no reason to defend an exclusive interpretation of his faith or any faith.

To underscore this point, Martel has Pi share a story drawn from Hindu tradition about the widely worshiped Lord Krishna, the eighth avatar or incarnation of one of the major Hindu deities, Vishnu, the Preserver. Pi says:

> But we should not cling! A plague upon fundamentalists and literalists! I am reminded of a story of Lord Krishna when he was a cowherd. Every night he invites the milkmaids to dance with him in the forest. They come and they dance. The night is dark, the fire in their midst roars and crackles, the beat of the music gets ever faster—the girls dance and dance and dance with their sweet lord, who has made himself so abundant as to be in the arms of each and every girl. But the moment the girls become possessive, the moment each one imagines that Krishna is her partner alone, He vanishes. So it is that we should not be jealous of God. (2001, 49)

Later Martel has Pi react to some of the more-zealous representatives of the religions he encountered. Pi says:

There are always those who take it upon themselves to defend God, as if Ultimate Reality, as if the sustaining frame of existence, were something weak and helpless. These people walk by a widow deformed by leprosy begging for a few paise [Indian coins], walk by children dressed in rags living in the street, and they think, "Business as usual." But if they perceive a slight against God, it is a different story. Their faces go red, their chests heave mightily, they sputter angry words. The degree of their indignation is astonishing. Their resolve is frightening.

These people fail to realize that it is on the inside that God must be defended, not on the outside. They should direct their anger at themselves. For evil in the open is but evil from within that has been let out. The main battlefield for good is not the open ground of the public arena but the small clearing of each heart. Meanwhile, the lot of widows and homeless children is very hard, and it is to their defence, not God's, that the self-righteous should rush. . . .

As if this small-mindedness did God any good. To me, religion is about our dignity, not our depravity. (70–71)

One need not agree with all that Pi says, but his critique of religion as practiced by many is on target. The question is, of course, how might we go about altering the misunderstanding of religious devotion that prompted Pi's reaction? The problem is at least twofold. First, as mentioned in the previous chapter, Christians need to reconsider the theological tradition of exclusivism that has provided the mind-set and encouragement for prejudice and intolerance. That reexamination has begun, but much remains to be done. But second, the level of ignorance among Christians about other religions is enormous. As part of the reevaluation of our theology, we need to learn more—much more—about the religious thought of others. Coincidentally, learning about the religion of another is extraordinarily helpful in helping one understand one's own religion.

This gap in knowledge and experience has to be bridged. But how? If we wait until we, or our people, know all that we/they need to know, we will never get started. So, let's take small steps. There are a number of strategies that might be utilized in helping our people come to such an awareness and appreciation. Some are "negative," things not to do. But most are "positive," I hope, things we can do that will help our people come to an appreciative understanding about who we really are and how we are to live in this world. Contextual interpretation is what we are about.

First, there is the avenue of discourse with others. The goal is never to "evangelize" the other but to get to know the other, what they think, what they believe, what is at the heart of their understanding and commitment to God. Try arranging with a local rabbi or imam or Hindu religious teacher for a conversation between members of your congregation and members of theirs. Part of the program, of course, is socializing, just getting the opportunity to meet with other people in the wider community and to do so as self-consciously "religious" folk. There should be a topic upon which to center the conversation. Perhaps films or plays may provide a place to begin. Or the topic might be something more explicitly "religious." I know of one congregation, for instance, that for a month discussed the topic "the sacred" with a neighboring Jewish congregation. What does "the sacred" signify to different groups? How is "the sacred" symbolized and acknowledged? Does any one religion have a corner on "the sacred"? Such conversations may begin rather shallowly, but as trust develops and conversations continue, real transformation can result.

Another avenue to explore is a common work project. A group from one congregation I know has joined with members of a neighboring mosque on a Habitat for Humanity project. Another sent a team of its members along with members of a neighboring Jewish synagogue to New Orleans to assist in the ongoing cleanup and rebuilding work made necessary by Hurricane Katrina. In each of these projects, Christians got to know Muslim and Jewish neighbors in a new way and gained a greater appreciation for how God can work through a variety of people. The sometimes-obtrusive character of doctrine often gives way before shared labors and common cause.

If you live near one of the now-several Holocaust museums in our country, you might arrange for a joint visit and follow-up discussion with people drawn from various religious communities in your town. And international travel that takes people to countries where other religious traditions are dominant can be very informative, if a serious effort is made to meet and learn from leaders of the religious traditions being encountered. By the way, while you are in Japan, for instance, talk with some of the Christians there and consider what it means to live in the midst of a country where Christians constitute but 1 percent of the population.

In recent years a very popular education project by Christian congregations has been to create a "first-century Jewish village" as a way to study the Jewish setting of the stories about Jesus. Shops, households, schools, synagogues, and so forth are erected so that the children (and their adult leaders as well, I dare say) can "experience" something of Jesus' childhood. These villages provide an educational opportunity to involve Jews from the local community as consultants who can bring added authenticity. If you want to hear the shofar (the ceremonial ram's horn) sounded, let a Jew trained for such occasions do the honors. If you want to make use of some Jewish symbols or some Hebrew words, let a Jew help in preparing them, both for accuracy and also for the opportunity to get to know your neighbors in the community.

A slight variation of this project is to construct a Hindu temple or Muslim mosque, with the help, of course, of local Hindus and Muslims. A visit before hand to a temple or mosque would be most instructive. Then by trying to replicate the experience for other children and adults in the congregation, everyone will learn all the more. If there are no Jews or Muslims or Hindus living near you, check with regional offices of the various faith traditions and see who and what might be available "on loan" as a resource.

A word of warning. When presenting Easter Passion Plays, take care how you present the Judean officials who were opposed to Jesus. To the degree that "Jews" in general and contemporary "Jews" in particular are made to appear as villains, a disservice, false witness, has been done. Stereotypes are to be avoided! All Pharisees were not wicked hypocrites. Most were honorable people, and some became followers of Jesus. All Jews were not and are not "Shylocks" and should not be so portrayed.

A similar warning concerning "Christian" seder meals is in order. If you want to better understand the seder (the Jewish meal associated with Passover), invite some Jews to come in and explain it. This is not a liturgical tradition that Christians should simply "take over" and claim as their own. The Lord's Supper, the Last Supper, whatever one may call it, was not a Jewish seder, and Christians should not try to claim it as such. The point is that special traditions of different religions should be honored and not "cannibalized" by those of other faiths.

Some joint projects may be more "controversial." Working together addressing issues of religion in the public schools or joining in efforts to have the death penalty reviewed requires greater risk. Working together to help a public school administration or faculty become more sensitive to the fact that the school homecoming day should not be scheduled in conflict with a major Jewish or Muslim or Hindu holy day—or Christian celebration for that matter—may provoke some hostility. Be sure to work together on such projects, however, to make certain that everyone involved understands the purpose and recognizes the pitfalls. Misunderstanding lurks like the proverbial lion at the gate, waiting to pounce on even the best of our efforts at interfaith sensitivity.

Another more ambitious project is the establishment of some form of interfaith council or forum in your community. There are a number of examples around. The one with which I am most familiar is located in Louisville, Kentucky, where I live. It has had several formats in the past thirty years and has evolved to bring together a number of different groups. The Roman Catholic Cathedral Heritage Foundation is the immediate predecessor and most instrumental source for the present organization that operates under the name The Center for Interfaith Relations. The CIR is "dedicated to promoting and supporting interfaith understanding, cooperation, and action." (For more information and a number of Internet links with other interfaith groups, see the CIR Homepage: www.interfaithrelations.org.) Its byword is, "Many Faiths, One Heart, Common Action." The program is built around three basic convictions:

1. The Divine is present in all persons and in their religious traditions.
2. Members of religious traditions are enriched by interfaith interactions and cooperation.
3. The community is enriched when members of religious traditions bring their faith and beliefs to civic life, houses of worship embrace their civic responsibility to the surrounding community, and houses of worship use their facilities for interfaith interaction and cooperation.

One recent event provides a good example of the work that CIR is doing in Louisville. It was called Faith Leaders' Forum and brought together some one hundred faith leaders for an all-day consultation "designed as both an occasion for faith leaders to meet and get to know each other across faith traditions and an opportunity to self-identify causes and concerns worthy of further attention by these leaders." The day unfolded with a number of table conversations around suggested questions. The makeup of each table group (four being the optimal number) changed every forty minutes so that by the end of the day each person had had the opportunity to meet a number of new people. Liturgical music was provided by representatives of four different faith traditions to help set the context. At the end of the day, observations and suggestions were gathered from the participants concerning "next steps." The event was considered a "success" by those who attended and follow-up forums are already being planned.

The CIR, building on the work of its predecessor, the Cathedral Heritage Foundation, has another very successful interfaith project called Festival of Faiths. The mission of the Festival is to celebrate the diversity of faiths in the community while expressing gratitude for our unity. The aim is to strengthen the role of all faith traditions in our society. In the course of this event, many different people in the community representing a wide variety of Christian and non-Christian traditions come together in meaningful conversation, with the valuable sharing of beliefs and concerns.

This is a weeklong event that involves numerous presentations by a variety of speakers and groups at a number of different venues. The visual and performing arts complement the more-usual lecture formats. Many of the presenters are drawn from the local community, but there are always some from the larger national and international arena. This provides all with the stimulation generated by recognized leaders and thinkers from various traditions from around the world. The offerings are planned by an interfaith committee and provide opportunity for all participants to contribute to the theme for the year from their faith tradition. The twelfth annual festival, held in November 2007, was the second in a series centering on different stages of life. The first, in 2006, considered various ways different religious traditions approached the issues of death and dying. The theme for 2007 was "Birth and Creation through the Eyes of Faith." In 2008 the topic was "Coming of Age," and in 2009, "Marriage." Over sixty thousand visitors have attended the Festival across the years since its inception in 1995.

The possibilities are endless. The aim is to enable Christians to recognize the new context of diversity into which God, I believe, is moving us. The way we read and interpret Scripture, the way we develop and articulate our theology, the way we worship, the way we move in our wider civil communities—all must be reconsidered in light of this new context. Part of this reconsideration, as we have been suggesting, requires learning about others in an empathetic and not merely critical manner. Our hearts as well as our minds must be restructured; face-to-face experience along with book learning is necessary.

A friend recently drew to my attention a vignette from a book that discusses the teaching behind and the process of participating in the daily practice of prayer as understood in the Sufi tradition, *Illuminated Prayer,* by Coleman Barks and Michael Green. This beautifully illustrated book tries to help readers visualize something of the mystical teachings upon which the tradition is based. Obviously, mystical experience is necessarily private and individual, but the story that is told does help inform both the problems and the possibilities inherent in our present situation.

> When a child asked him one day what to say when asked what religion she was, Bawa [a Sufi master] gave another hint of how his community might understand itself:
> You are a Christian because you believe in Jesus and you are a Jew because you believe in all the prophets including Moses. You are a Muslim because you believe in Muhammad as a prophet and you are a Sufi because you believe in the universal teaching of God's love. You are really none of those, but you are all of those because you believe in God. And once you believe in God there is no religion. Once you divide yourself off with religion you are separated from your fellowman. (2000, 14)

The "old" way of doing business is simply no longer adequate to the task. The theological task will take considerable time, but it is beginning and needs to be supported. The educational goal will always be a moving target. There is so much to learn about others and about ourselves. Each new encounter demonstrates how much remains to be done. The learning that is promoted needs to be cognitive, certainly, but even more, it needs to be experiential and involve the whole range of our senses. People learning shoulder to shoulder with others, Christians and non-Christians, is what is needed.

But all the lectures and books and workshops in the world cannot finally do what has to be done. That has to be done at the local level by local leaders with the everyday people who make up our communities. We cannot afford to keep putting this off as if it is merely an "extra" that would be interesting if we had nothing else to do. We all have many things to do, but the challenge of the next twenty years requires that we prepare ourselves and our people. Opening the eyes and ears of good folk like my mom is the name of the game!

Discussion Questions

1. What are some ways that you and your congregation might begin to meet and learn about some people of another faith? What types of discussions or sharing would be useful and possible? Who do you know in your community that might be willing to help?
2. How can leaders in your wider community be brought together to make efforts at enabling people to learn about those of different religions? What are some of the more obvious difficulties? How might a council or a study group dedicated to dealing with the varieties of religious expression in your community be useful?
3. Why is it important to combine emotional experience with rational study? What kinds of knowledge can best be obtained through direct encounter with others? How does theology try to help us organize our thinking about such matters?

Chapter Twelve

Reaching Out

*M*artin E. Marty, noted historian and keen observer of the American religious scene, in his recent volume *When Faiths Collide* has provided an important reminder for those who recognize the reality of religious pluralism and the necessity for dealing with it. He comments:

> Metaphysicians may debate, preachers may thunder, leaders may jostle for position, but, there being no arbiter on the scene and no means of providing access to the source of truth among the claims of religions, citizens have to combine their own commitment to "their truth," which they may see as "the truth" and find ways to live creatively with those who offer insights "incommensurable" to their own. On such a basis, they seek civil peace, the kind of peace one needs for public life, even if it is not finally metaphysically satisfying. (2005, 155)

The issues addressed in Marty's volume, and raised in this book as well, will not be easily or quickly resolved, but we can make a beginning.

Akbar Ahmed, mentioned in the previous chapter, adds additional warning as he succinctly summarizes the current situation with regard to some of the turmoil many currently experience in our religious and cultural diversity:

> What lies at the core of all great world faiths is clearly missing in today's world: a sense of justice, compassion, and knowledge. The tidal wave of globalization has swept over the world with economic and financial might, fomenting anger, greed, and ignorance. In such an environment, feelings of compassion and understanding for others become irrelevant—human beings and human relation-

ships do not appear to matter. This characteristic of globalization has been accelerated since 9/11. Learned professors of law—those who should know better—have justified the use of torture in its most degrading forms in secret prison camps. The U.S. war on terror has become a distorted symbol of globalization associated with torture and the suspension of human rights to millions of the poor and dispossessed and those who feel for them. This challenges the naïve, ethnocentric assumption of Western intellectuals that globalization promotes "cosmopolitan tolerance" and that this is a characteristic of Western culture that can now be transmitted to the rest of the world. The human race is at the point of losing what makes it human: compassion. It needs to rediscover compassion for every one of its social units, from immediate kin to the larger societies that share this planet. (2007, 46–47)

One further contribution to be noted here is from Robert J. Nash in *Religious Pluralism in the Academy*. In describing some "ground rules" for productive dialogue, he wrote:

The golden rule of moral conversation is a willingness to find the truth in what we oppose and the error in what we espouse, before we presume to acknowledge the truth in what we espouse and the error in what we oppose. (2001, 178)

Such is exceedingly difficult to do, but extraordinarily important to attempt.

This is the situation in which we find ourselves. Real frustration is stirred up when we have to deal with the reality of diversity. It is difficult to comprehend and adjust to all of the diversity encountered at the international level, but in some ways it is perhaps even more so when the diversity is local. Differences of opinion—especially on maters of religion—abound! Sometimes we just don't want to think about it. Sometimes we deny the reality of it. But in the long run, we will have to deal with it, because ethnic, political, sexual, religious diversity is here, and as much as some of us might want it to disappear, it is not going to go away.

The only pertinent question is how we are going to deal with it. Are we going to see diversity as a divine gift or a satanic curse? Personally, I consider pluralism, and all the wondrous differences that go with it, to be a marvelous gift from God. I consider the religious diversity we are now coming to know firsthand to be part of God's ongoing, gracious providence. We live in a wonderfully varied world and should rejoice and be glad. But I acknowledge Martin Marty's words of caution:

> Advocacy of conversation does not always produce positive results. Learning limits of conversation within pluralism is essential. . . . All the good will in the world will not bring concord in many cases. Yet, in a world of prejudice and civil chaos, of war and terrorism, efforts to understand what happens when faiths collide can be the first step in minimizing the damage. (2005, 123)

Nonetheless, dialogue, informed conversation, is what we must pursue, among ourselves and with others beyond our tribe. For Protestant (and perhaps all) Christians, the first place to begin is with the Bible and its interpretation. I have made a start in this endeavor with my book *The Wide, Wide Circle of Divine Love* (2005) and have continued that exploration in the pages of this volume. It is clear to me that the Bible suggests that the human family, the whole human family, is one under God. Only "majorities" are tempted to think that they alone matter before God. What we are coming to realize ever more clearly is that Christians, Jews, Muslims—all constitute minorities when placed in our shared context of the world's population. None of us are God's "only" people. We are all part of a beautiful tapestry that God is weaving. Our challenge is to recognize our place in the divine masterpiece.

When interpreted against its original historical context and in its contemporary social context, the Bible is incredibly inclusive. God's invitation to participate in the fullness of divine love extends to all. And God's expectation is expressly declared that each of us should love one another. Christians are explicitly enjoined to love others, both others in the community of the church but especially others who are enemies (Matthew 5:43–48; Mark 12:28–34; Luke 6:27–36; John 13:34–35). One can hardly be more inclusive than that.

We have reflected upon passages drawn from a number of places in the Bible. It is clear that God's people often have not understood correctly what God intended. Exhortations to repentance are found in both the First and the Second Testaments, but always in the context of assurances of divine love and mercy. The contributions of those outside Israel and outside the church have been noted, signaling at least that God has been engaged with people around the globe since the beginning of the human story. Even the most jarring of biblical texts—passages that are clearly "harsh"—are seen to have a much more particular and specific intent when read against the original historical context. Particular instructions for particular situations are what we find rather than the absolute, universal propositions that too many for too long have assumed. There is frequent witness to the One who is true, but few abstract declarations of "the truth." But, regrettably, that is not how most Christians have been taught to read the Bible, least of all my mom.

If there is going to be a change that will be helpful for people like my mother, something else must accompany the renewed consideration of the Bible. There is a fundamental theological reorientation that is also necessary. If one comes to the Bible with the belief that it is intended only for the "insiders," then that is what one will find. Thus, it is critical for the church to give renewed consideration to a proper understanding of the place of the "other."

Paul Knitter, Roman Catholic scholar and theologian, in *Introducing Theologies of Religions* urges the recognition of what he calls the Acceptance Model. This approach has been emerging during the past two decades and offers a fourth option beyond the models mentioned earlier in chapter 1. Knitter's nomenclature for these other approaches in Christian theology is the Replacement Model (i.e., Exclusivist), the Fulfillment Model (i.e., Inclusivist), and the Mutuality Model (i.e., Pluralist). Commenting on the usual approaches, Knitter says:

> [They] either so stress the particularity of one religion that the validity of all others is jeopardized (the Replacement and the Fulfillment Models) or they stress the universal validity of them all in a way that fogs over the real particular differences (the Mutuality Model). What we are calling the Acceptance Model thinks it can do a better job at this balancing act. And, as we will see, it does so not by holding up the superiority of any one religion, nor by searching for that common something that makes them all valid, but by accepting the real diversity of all faiths. The religious traditions of the world are really different, and we have to *accept* those differences. (2002, 173)

The particularity of each religious tradition is critical to maintain, but this must be done with the understanding that the distinctiveness of each faith tradition is equally important. This need is underscored by E. David Cook. When commenting on the work of John Hick and Paul Knitter, he notes:

> This move stems from the practical experience of Christians who are experiencing pluralism in a new way. It is not just feeling the reality of other religious paths, but also their vitality, their influence on the modern world and their depth, beauty and attractiveness. This new experience is leading Christians to feel the need for a more productive dialogue and cooperation with other religions. Christians need to have a new attitude toward other religions. (1992, 238)

Thus, along with a renewal of biblical study and sensitivity to the way others articulate their faith, Christians will have to become far clearer concerning their own theology. What are the distinctive stories that differentiate Christians from other religious people? What beliefs are essential and which are nonessential? If, as our biblical study suggests, God has chosen to be present with peoples all around the world and has revealed the divine will through and to others, then how are Christians to understand their own place before God and the distinctive contribution they are expected to make?

This is no easy task. Agreement will never be fully reached. Nevertheless, this is part of the task before us. The two most critical issues, it seems to me, revolve around the person of Jesus of Nazareth and the mission he gave to his disciples. Now the church has wrestled with the first of these issues since the very beginning of the Christian movement. The Gospel of Mark, for instance, has no birth story, whereas Matthew (1:18–25) and Luke (1:26–38) ascribe Jesus' birth to the Virgin Mary. The Gospel of John (1:1–4, 14–18) relates no account of the birth of Jesus but rather equates Jesus with the Word of God that was present with God before the world was ever created. The Letters of the apostle Paul are the earliest documents preserved in the New Testament. Paul wrote of Jesus only that he was "born of a woman" (Galatians 4:4). Various leaders and thinkers have debated the "essential" character of the doctrine of "virgin birth" almost from the beginning.

Claims for the supernatural and/or virginal conception of the leader of a tradition are not unique to Christianity. There were those who believed that Plato the philosopher was born of a virgin. Similar stories circulated concerning Alexander the Great and later, Caesar Augustus. The tradition of Jesus' virgin birth in the earliest centuries of the church was used to emphasize Jesus' humanity, not his divinity. It was critical to the early church to make certain that people understood that Jesus was a real human being and not some phantom that only appeared to be flesh and blood.

The formal doctrine of the Trinity that, among other things, aimed at resolving questions concerning Christ's "dual nature" (truly human and truly divine) and the internal relationship between "Father, Son, and Holy Spirit," was not clearly articulated until the fourth and fifth centuries CE. It was an extremely sophisticated explication intended to make the biblical stories about Jesus compatible with the dominant philosophy (Neoplatonism) of the day. This doctrine continues to prompt debate in the church whenever explanations of its meaning are required.

Now these are only two of the beliefs that help define Christianity. Depending upon the branch of the church one examines, many more distinct teachings can be found. But within all of this diversity, there are at least two features of the story that practically all Christians agree upon: (1) Jesus Christ is Lord and has defeated the power of death, and (2) everyone baptized in Jesus' name belongs in some way to the Christian movement. These two convictions are "essential" in telling the Christian story. They set Christians apart from those of other faith traditions. To be able to converse seriously within our fellowship and with those outside the Christian tradition requires that we become clear in our own minds what we do in fact believe and why, and cultivate ways of sharing these things with others.

Such sharing takes us to the second major issue: What is the mission of the church? In recent centuries the mission was assumed to be the conversion of the people of the world to Christianity. This was not of special importance during the centuries we designate as the Medieval Period because in the places where Christianity was primarily situated, Christians were the majority. Contact with adherents of other religions was modest at best. But as the Modern Period began to unfold, greater contact with "outsiders" began to occur. Further, as several of the nations of Europe came to be world powers, the need arose to "Christianize" the "natives" in conquered lands. Converging with this concern was a growing conviction that the "end of the age" (and with it the full reign of God in this world) could only come to pass when all peoples had been exposed to the gospel. Thus the mission was defined as "taking Christ to the world."

Recent biblical study now suggests that this understanding of the work of the church is based on a misunderstanding of passages like that in Matthew 28:19–20, often called the Great Commission. Jesus' followers, those who call him Lord, are indeed expected to witness to the power of Jesus' love in their lives and on behalf of the world. We are to invite people to join us as disciples of Jesus Christ. But our primary work is witnessing to our belief that in Jesus the reign of God has broken into this world.

We have already been granted a glimpse of the wholeness, the peace, the justice, that God intends in this world. We are witnesses to this wonderful inbreaking and are asked to live our lives differently in light of what God has done, and will do, in Jesus Christ. Any who wish to join in this work are to be welcomed joyfully as compatriots in discipleship. But it is not our task to "convert" the world. Jesus' disciples are like salt or like yeast. We are a light in the world, not the sun. We will always be "small" because that is the way we work best. We aren't expected to constitute the "majority," and history shows us that we have often been at our worst when we did have too many in numbers or too much in the way of civil power.

Martin Marty ends his "manifesto" *When Faiths Collide* with a word of caution and challenge. He encourages Christians to adopt the practice of hospitality more fully into their approach to the "others," in the effort to engage them in the midst of religious pluralism. But there are risks and limitations to the risk-taking approach he encourages. While the development of theologies of pluralism advanced by some liberal thinkers may be worthy, Marty thinks, the likelihood of their winning wide acceptance is not great. But that is no reason to give up. In illustrating his point, Marty refers to the work of Marc Gopin concerning the conflict in the Middle East (2002, 198ff.). Gopin recognized how important religious constructs are in the public arena and how they must be acknowledged. Cultures are dynamic. Marty then quotes Gopin:

> We must bring the issues of peace and conflict into innovative spaces of human engagement, such as the street, the public space, an area that has been engaged historically by cultural and religious traditions but is utterly neglected by the abstractions of contemporary approaches to coexistence. The public space matters. The human face in the public space matters.

Marty thus concludes:

> So long as the human face is welcomed in the public space, there is life. Faiths will continue to collide, but those individuals and groups that risk hospitality and promote engagement with the stranger, the different, the other, will contribute to a world in which measured hope can survive and those who hope can guide. (2005, 178)

I have suggested a tapestry as a useful metaphor for considering God's work in the world. So far as the tapestry is concerned, each thread is important. Each in its own distinctiveness, its own color, its own texture, makes a significant contribution to the whole. The aim is not to reduce each thread to a bland, neutral, look-alike of all the other threads. Not at all! Each religious tradition has its own distinct makeup, which complements the whole. God's creative power brings it all together. What is needed is for each tradition to recognize what it has to offer to the whole and to do so clearly and powerfully.

This is a metaphor that I think my mother might have understood. To be able to make the contribution expected of us, we must commit ourselves to becoming better informed about our own religion and to engaging in honest, open dialogue with those of other faiths. We will have to open our eyes and recognize the new context in which we now are challenged to witness as Jesus' disciples. The Bible requires new interpretation appropriate to the new situation. And it can't be only with our heads. It must also involve our hearts. Our intellects will need to be informed by empathy as well as by "the facts." My mom wanted to know how the tradition came to be as it is and why some of the critical details of its development had not been shared with her. Clarity and honest sharing is the task. It is difficult, but it is not impossible.

Discussion Questions

1. What are some of the "dangers" or "difficulties" that arise when people try to deal with questions of religious pluralism? How can such concerns be honored without letting them rule out discussion or cooperation? What steps can be taken to lessen the problems?

2. What are some of the essentials about the Christian faith that should not be cast aside or toned down when Christians share their faith with others? In what ways has contemporary biblical and theological research suggested that some of the essentials have been misunderstood?

3. Why is it critical that Christians begin to reach out to others in ways different from the past? What are some of the "new" aspects of our context that seem to make this engagement more important than it has been? What is the mission of the church in our new context?

Reference List

Entries in bold type are suggestions for additional reading.

Ahmed, Akbar S. 2007. *Journey into Islam: The Crisis of Globalization.* **Washington, DC: Brookings Institution Press.**

Aponte, David, and Migues A. De La Torre. 2006. *Handbook of Latina/o Theologies.* St. Louis: Chalice Press.

Barks, Coleman, and Michael Green. 2000. *Illuminated Prayer.* New York: Ballantine Wellspring.

Bevans, Stephen B. 1992. *Models of Contextual Theology.* Maryknoll, NY: Orbis.

Bonney, Richard. 2004. *Jihad: From Qur'an to bin Laden.* New York: Palgrave Macmillan.

Campbell, Cynthia M. 2007. *A Multitude of Blessings: A Christian Approach to Religious Diversity.* Louisville, KY: Westminster John Knox Press.

Carroll, James. 2001. *Constantine's Sword: The Church and the Jews.* Boston: Houghton Mifflin.

Chung, Paul S., Veli-Matti Kärkkäinen, and Kim Kyoung-Jae, eds. 2007. *Asian Contextual Theology for the Third Millennium: A Theology of Minjung in the Fourth-Eye Formation.* Eugene, OR: Pickwick Publications.

Cook, E. David. 1992. "Truth, Mystery, and Justice: Hick and Christianity's Uniqueness." In *One God, One Lord: Christianity in a World of Religious Pluralism,* ed. Andrew D. Clarke and Bruce W. Winter. Grand Rapids: Baker Book House.

Dahood, Mitchell. 1966. *Psalms I: 1–50.* Anchor Bible. Garden City, NY: Doubleday.

Diamond, Jared. 1997. *Guns, Germs, and Steel: The Fates of Human Societies.* New York and London: W. W. Norton.

Driver, G. R. 1956. *Canaanite Myths and Legends.* Edinburgh: T&T Clark.

Eck, Diana. 1993. *Encountering God: A Spiritual Journey from Bozeman to Banaras.* Boston: Beacon.

———. 2001. *A New Religious America: How a "Christian Country" Has Become the World's Most Religiously Diverse Nation.* San Francisco: HarperSanFrancisco.

111

Friedman, Thomas L. 2005. *The World Is Flat: A Brief History of the Twenty-First Century.* New York: Farrar, Girard & Straus.

Gopin, Marc. 2002. *Holy War, Holy Peace: How Religion Can Bring Peace to the Middle East.* New York: Oxford University Press.

Hillers, D. R. 1972. *Covenant: The History of a Biblical Idea.* Baltimore: Johns Hopkins Press.

Jenkins, Philip. 2002. *The Next Christendom: The Coming of Global Christianity.* Oxford: Oxford University Press.

Jinkins, Michael. 2004. *Christianity, Tolerance, and Pluralism: A Theological Engagement with Isaiah Berlin's Social Theory.* London and New York: Routledge.

Knitter, Paul F. 2002. *Introducing Theologies of Religions.* Maryknoll, NY: Orbis Books.

Levine, Amy-Jill. 2006. *The Misunderstood Jew: The Church and the Scandal of the Jewish Jesus.* San Francisco: HarperSanFrancisco. Adapted as "Misusing Jesus." *Christian Century,* December 26, 2006.

March, W. Eugene. 2005. *The Wide, Wide Circle of Divine Love.* Louisville, KY: Westminster John Knox Press.

———. 2007. *Great Themes of the Bible.* Louisville, KY: Westminister John Knox Press.

Martel, Yann. 2001. *Life of Pi: A Novel.* Orlando, FL: Harcourt.

Marty, Martin E. 2005. *When Faiths Collide.* Oxford: Blackwell.

McCarthy, D. J. 1972. *Old Testament Covenant.* Atlanta: John Knox Press.

Nash, Robert J. 2001. *Religious Pluralism in the Academy: Opening the Dialogue.* New York: Peter Lang.

Pawlikowski, John T. 1994. "Christian Theological Concerns after the Holocaust." In *Visions of the Other: Jewish and Christian Theologians Assess the Dialogue,* ed. Eugene J. Fisher, 28–51. Mahwah, NJ: Paulist Press.

Pitts, Leonard. 2007. Column in *The Courier Journal.* Louisville, KY. December 9.

Pritchard, James B., ed. 1955. *Ancient Near Eastern Texts Relating to the Old Testament.* 2nd ed. Princeton, NJ: Princeton University Press.

Quammen, David. 2003. *Monster of God: The Man-Eating Predator in the Jungles of History and the Mind.* New York and London: W. W. Norton.

Sacks, Jonathan. 2003. *The Dignity of Difference: How to Avoid the Clash of Civilizations.* Rev. ed. London and New York: Continuum.

Sanneh, Lamin, and Joel Carpenter, eds. 2005. *The Changing Face of Christianity: Africa, the West, and the World.* Oxford: Oxford University Press.

Tamez, Elsa. 2002. "Reading the Bible under a Sky without Stars." In *The Bible in a World Context: An Experiment in Contextual Hermeneutics,* ed. Walter Dietrich and Ulrich Luz, 3–16. Grand Rapids: Eerdmans.

Torres Queiruga, Andrés, Luiz Carlos Susin, and José Maria Vigil, eds. 2007. *Pluralist Theology: The Emerging Paradigm.* London: SCM Press.

Weigel, George. 2007. *Faith, Reason, and the War against Jihadism.* Garden City, NY: Doubleday.

Wilfred, Felix. 1995. *From the Dusty Soil: Contextual Reinterpretation of Christianity.* Tambaram: University of Madras.

Wit, Hans de, et al., eds. 2004. *Through the Eyes of Another: Intercultural Reading of the Bible*. Elkhart, IN: Institute of Mennonite Studies.

Zangenberg, Jürgen, and Michael Labahn, eds. 2004. *Christians as a Religious Minority in a Multicultural City*. London and New York: T&T Clark.